How to Learn A
and Change your Life in the Process

FLUENT
F OR
FREE

MARIA SPANTIDI

Copyright © 2020 by **Maria Spantidi**

Fluent For Free

All rights reserved. No part of this publication may be reproduced, distributed or transmitted in any form or by any means, including photocopying, recording, or other electronic or mechanical methods, without the prior written permission of the publisher, except in the case of brief quotations embodied in critical reviews and certain other noncommercial uses permitted by copyright law.

The information contained in this book is the opinion of the author and is based on the author's personal experiences and observations. The author and publisher of this book make no representation or warranties with respect to the accuracy, applicability or completeness of the contents of this book. The information contained in this book is strictly for educational purposes. Therefore, if you wish to apply ideas contained in this book, you are taking full responsibility for your actions. Any perceived slight of any individual or organization is purely unintentional.

Cover Design by 100Covers.com
Interior Design by FormattedBooks.com

*You live a new life for every new language you speak.
If you know only one language, you live only once.*

—Czech proverb

CONTENTS

INTRODUCTION: WHY I WROTE THIS BOOK IX
    WHO IS THIS BOOK FOR? XIX
    WHO IS THIS BOOK NOT FOR? XIX
    HOW TO USE THIS BOOK XXI

SECTION 1. GETTING STARTED – DEVELOPING YOUR MINDSET 1
    WHAT'S STOPPING YOU? BUSTING COMMON LANGUAGE LEARNING MYTHS 3
        MYTH #1: I DON'T HAVE THE TALENT FOR LANGUAGE LEARNING 4
        MYTH #2: I DON'T HAVE TIME TO LEARN A LANGUAGE! 6
        MYTH #3: I'M TOO OLD TO LEARN A LANGUAGE! 7
        MYTH #4: I'M TOO SHY TO LEARN A LANGUAGE! 8
        MYTH #5: TO LEARN A LANGUAGE, I HAVE TO TRAVEL TO THE COUNTRY
            WHERE IT'S SPOKEN. 9
        MYTH #6: SUCCESSFUL LANGUAGE LEARNERS AND POLYGLOTS SPEND
            TOO MUCH TIME STUDYING. 10
        MYTH #7: LANGUAGE LEARNING IS EXPENSIVE! 10
        MYTH #8: I'M NOT SMART ENOUGH TO LEARN A LANGUAGE! 11
        MYTH #9: THERE'S A PERFECT METHOD FOR EVERYONE! 12
    SETTING YOUR FLUENCY FOUNDATIONS 15
    BREAKING DOWN LANGUAGES 22
    TRAIN YOUR BRAIN - A NEW MENTALITY 29
        NECESSITY STIMULATES CREATIVITY 29

SECTION 2. FREE METHODS AND RESOURCES 33
    COLLECTING MATERIAL ON THE INTERNET - CRITERIA AND APPROACHES 35
    VOCABULARY 42
        REPETITION, REPETITION, REPETITION 43
        FLASHCARDS 44
        ANKI 45
        MEMRISE 45
        DUOLINGO 46
        CLOZEMASTER 46

- BECOMING THE MASTER OF YOUR SRS 47
- STICKY NOTES 48
- CONTEXT CLUES 49
- THE MOST COMMON WORDS 50
- STORYTELLING 51
- MNEMONICS 51
- BE CREATIVE AND HAVE FUN! 52
- BRAINSTORMING 53
- MAKE YOUR OWN SENTENCES 53
- I'VE HEARD THAT BEFORE! - COGNATES 54
- GOOGLE TRANSLATE 55
- USE MEDIA 55
- USE YOUR SENSES 56
- USE SOCIAL MEDIA 56
- GENERAL VOCABULARY TIPS 57

GRAMMAR 61
- FEEL THE GRAMMAR 62
- TWO-WAY TRANSLATION 66
- HAVE NATIVE SPEAKERS COMPLETE THE SENTENCES FOR YOU 67
- WORDREFERENCE FORUMS 69
- WHAT ABOUT VERB TABLES? 69
- WHAT ABOUT IRREGULAR VERBS? 70

LISTENING 71
- LISTENING EXPLAINED 72
- HOW TO IMPROVE YOUR LISTENING SKILLS 73
- CHOOSING LISTENING MATERIAL 75
- YOUTUBE 75
- TED TALKS 77
- MUSIC 77
- PODCASTS 78
- ONLINE RADIO 78
- IMPROVING YOUR LISTENING SKILLS DURING A REAL CONVERSATION 79
- I DON'T UNDERSTAND NATIVE SPEAKERS! 80

READING 84
- HOW TO TURN ANY WEBPAGE INTO LANGUAGE LEARNING MATERIAL 86
- READING EXPLAINED 87
- PICKING READING TOPICS 88
- FINDING READING MATERIALS 89
- WHEN YOUR TARGET LANGUAGE MEETS YOUR OWN LANGUAGE 91
- BOOKS AND BIG TEXTS 91
- READING IS A NATURAL SRS 92
- READING FOR ADVANCED LEARNERS 92

- OTHER READING TIPS 94
- **SPEAKING** 95
  - FINDING A LANGUAGE PARTNER 97
  - ITALKI 97
  - INTERPALS 98
  - LANGUAGE EXCHANGE 98
  - WHAT TO DO BEFORE AND DURING A CONVERSATION WITH A NATIVE SPEAKER 99
  - LANGUAGE CAFES 100
  - GETTING CORRECTED 101
  - TALKING TO YOURSELF 102
  - THE PHONE TRICK 108
  - HOW ABOUT A VIDEO? 112
  - LEARN FILLER WORDS 113
- **PRONUNCIATION** 114
  - INITIAL STEPS 116
  - SHADOWING 118
  - SHADOWING WITH MUSIC 120
  - HOW TO IMPROVE YOUR ACCENT THROUGH MUSIC 121
  - FINDING A MODEL SPEAKER 122
  - LEARNING TO PRONOUNCE WORDS CORRECTLY 123
  - DON'T TAKE IT TO THE EXTREME! - THE ACCENT TRAP 124
- **WRITING** 128
  - WRITE STUFF 130
  - WRITING COMMENTS 131
  - FINDING A WRITING PARTNER 131
  - REWRITE IT! 131
  - GETTING YOUR ESSAYS CORRECTED 132
  - WRITING SUMMARIES 133
  - START SMALL 134
  - SHORT STORIES 134
  - IMPROVING SPEAKING THROUGH WRITING 135
- BECOMING A POLYGLOT FOR FREE - STUDYING MORE THAN ONE LANGUAGE 137
- LINGUISTIC TERMS - DO I HAVE TO LEARN THEM? 139
- STUDYING FOR A LANGUAGE CERTIFICATE 143
- DID YOU FIND ANY COOL RESOURCE THAT'S NOT IN THIS BOOK? 147

SECTION 3. BECOMING THE LEADER - CREATING A LANGUAGE ROUTINE 149

- CHOOSING THE METHODS 151
- CREATING A LANGUAGE LEARNING PLAN 157
  - BREAKING BIG TASKS INTO SMALLER 161
  - THE POWER OF DOING SOMETHING EVERY DAY 163
- SAMPLE ROUTINE YOU CAN USE 167

MOTIVATION 172
    SMALL VICTORIES IN LANGUAGE LEARNING 173

SECTION 4. TROUBLESHOOTING 179

    LANGUAGE LEARNING FAILURES 181
    DOUBTING YOURSELF 189
    MAKING MISTAKES 192
    "I CAN'T GET BETTER!" - LEARNING PLATEAU 198
    "FINDING THE BEST METHODS FOR ME TAKES TOO MUCH TIME" 201
    "IT GETS BORING!" 203
    "I CAN DO BETTER, I SWEAR!" 206
    "I'VE NO IDEA WHAT I'M DOING!" 208
    "I'M NOT READY TO SPEAK TO PEOPLE!" 210
    WHEN ALL ELSE FAILS - HONEST SELF-QUESTIONING 213

CONCLUSION 217

INTRODUCTION: WHY I WROTE THIS BOOK

"A different language is a different vision of life."
—Federico Fellini

Although I speak eight languages at different levels, I'm not a language teacher or a linguistic expert. I've studied nothing even remotely related to foreign languages and language learning. In fact, I wasn't always fond of languages.

I got into language learning by accident.

People usually associate language learning with trying to cram information into your brain, memorize words, and perform grammar rule drills. That's exactly what I thought of it, too. I also deemed language learning as a waste of time and money.

There, I said it: I hated language learning at first. I thought it was boring—just another lesson in the school curriculum, one of those things I knew I had to do, but couldn't bring myself to do it. It was a bit like when you're young and your mother takes you to the dentist. You know you have to go or you'll end up with bad teeth, right?

But it *hurts*.

You know it hurts because you remember your last visit. Despite your mother telling you otherwise, you want to scream at the top of your lungs from the pain. So, naturally, you put your brain to work to come up with creative excuses why you shouldn't go.

That's exactly what I did with language learning in the beginning.

When I was at school, back in Greece, we had one compulsory subject called "second foreign language" (the first foreign language was English), and we had to choose between German and French. I didn't like either one, so I selected what I thought would be the lesser of two evils—French. Back then, German sounded way too harsh to my ears (Little did I know I'd eventually learn it and move to Germany! But more on that later).

My French teacher was good. She made us play with verb conjugations and sing songs in French; but because she also had to stick to the school curriculum, we mostly learned from a textbook. Boring! I did my best to get good grades, but I learned no French. The following year we had a teacher I didn't like, so I stopped paying attention to French altogether.

So after three years of French, I spoke no French at all, but I recalled only a phrase or two from the songs we used to sing. That was it! It was just another boring subject that finally ended.

The following years, we didn't have any compulsory foreign language lessons other than English, so all was good—all except my language skills.

In addition to my regular school, my parents sent me to a language school to learn English as a kid. Even though this took years and I found it daunting, it worked to an extent. I passed my final exam—but I failed repeatedly to speak the language in real situations (when I wasn't too shy to even attempt speaking it). I got scared to death every time someone mentioned I had to speak English to people.

For example, I recollect the summers I'd spend on the Greek island of Chios, having fun and playing with other children. As soon as tourists would come and play with us, I'd get so scared, wondering, *Does that mean we have to speak English? Oh, no!* I wouldn't understand much of what they'd say, so all I'd say would be "yes" from time to time. Secretly I prayed they'd leave, so I wouldn't have to speak it anymore.

Just like the dentist, language learning *hurt*.

Back then, languages meant one thing and one thing only to me: going to a language school and attending those tedious classes until I was ready to take some exams and confirm my competence in the language. I never thought there was another way. I didn't know any differently.

For these reasons, I rejected foreign languages altogether, swearing to myself I'd never have to do this again. Whenever someone asked whether I considered learning a new language, I'd come up with any excuse I could think of: *I'm not talented. I'm good at math, not languages. I can't afford it. Everyone speaks English and I understand that language, so there's no need to study another language.* You name it; I've used it as an excuse!

If they insisted I study another language, I'd answer, "I'm done with languages for now. I'll probably do it later." (If you're familiar with Greek culture, *later* usually means *never* or *Leave me alone. I'm giving you nothing to argue with me about. I said I'll do it, so stop asking me.*)

So how did I go from feeling that way about language learning to someone that can speak so many languages, someone who loves language learning so much? How did I radically change? What made me fall in love with language learning and let it change my life for good?

It wasn't easy. It took a long time.

In my first year of university in Greece, I still wanted to hear nothing about languages, but students there kept talking about them. That baffled me. *What? In an engineering department? Why? I'm here to become an engineer, not to learn languages!*

Lecturers, however, insisted that learning German would help me significantly in the engineering field, as many books and regulations are written in the language. Learning that language would push my career forward. That sounded interesting to me, since all I cared about at the time was becoming a great engineer.

But, if I wanted to learn German, that meant paying for language schools and taking exams. *Not that nightmare again!* I released a cry from deep inside me. Even if I passed the exams and finished the classes, I'd have to speak the language, just like in the past with those tourists during my summer vacations. Plus, it'd be too expensive for me.

I knew that learning German would be so important for my career, though, and that it'd help me stop being poor! So, as I was desperate, I tried to find a different way to learn German. I paid for a mail-order German course with textbooks: a coursebook, a workbook, a study companion full of vocabulary, and some exercises that I'd send every month to a German teacher, who would correct them and send them back to me. Basically, the difference was that I'd teach myself German instead of paying for a teacher.

Sounded like a plan!

I lasted only one month and finished the first three units of the textbooks. The first unit was about booking a flight, the second was about staying at a hotel, and the third was about furniture (or something like that). I found them so boring, but I put a lot of pressure on myself and did exactly what I was told. I had to master German!

After I sent the first set of exercises for correction, I waited. The corrected exercises came back to me.

Everything was *wrong*!

Even though I did everything the books instructed me to do and pushed forward to finish those uninteresting units, all my efforts were completely in vain. Everything!

I gave up instantly and never opened those books again. Once more, I'd failed at languages, and I started making up excuses again to cope with my incompetence: *"Oh, come on. It's not like I need German to become a good engineer. I need good engineering skills to become a good engineer! My skills will be so good that I won't ever have to learn German! Languages are for people who don't have good engineering skills!"*

I went to great lengths to justify my choice not to learn German.

The problem was that, as the semesters went by, I also lost interest in engineering. In fact, I started hating my university too. I skipped classes and spent a lot of time in my room doing nothing, feeling terrible about myself. I hated everything. I wanted out of my university. I thought I had no future and that I wasn't good enough at anything.

On top of that, the Greek financial crisis was here to stay. My mother lost her job, and I was also unemployed. The world didn't seem to make sense anymore. I started having panic attacks and losing my sleep.

Like many young Greeks during the financial crisis, I lived with my parents because I had no other realistic option, and I grew fearful of leaving my house, especially at night. Going clubbing or spending the night out was a big no-no for me. I was too scared to do that, and it didn't bother me that all the other students my age did it.

One day, just to stop thinking about all these things for a little while, my mother, my aunt, and I went to see a movie called *The Women on the 6th Floor*, which was about a traditional wealthy Frenchman who lived in an apartment in Paris and had a Spanish maid. That Spanish maid lived on the sixth floor of the same building with her colleagues, who were also Spanish.

When the Frenchman ascended that top floor, it turned out that the girls were having fun, speaking Spanish, and being nice to each other; in stark contrast with that serious, cold French guy.

This scene sparked something in me. These girls were so cool! They were speaking Spanish to each other, doing cool things, and enjoying life! Even though they were poor (just like me) and seemed to have no future (also like me), they seemed so happy!

The movie ended, and I thought, *Wouldn't it be amazing if I knew how to speak Spanish? When those girls in the movie speak it, it sounds so cool, so out of this world!*

Now, if I wanted to make a cheesy romantic story out of this, I'd say that I started to learn Spanish because of that movie and the way it made me feel, which would be a lie. Although I started to like Spanish because of that movie, I didn't start learning it at that time—it happened by accident a few months later.

I discovered a website, where I could play with a foreign language for free, and Spanish was the first option. I said, "Why not? Let's give it a try!" and I started testing the website.

In the meantime, as I aimlessly browsed the Internet, I discovered that there were people who could speak many languages and loved learning them. I was floored!

I thought, *Hey, there are people out there that love learning languages! I'm sure they don't sign up for language schools, do they? Don't tell me they love those tedious classes! They don't? Does that mean there's another way to learn languages? Is there something different out there?*

Combine those thoughts with that free language learning website I was playing, and my new interest was born. I started playing with Spanish for just a few minutes every day, gradually moving from that website to others, asking questions, watching funny videos, and trying to acquire as much as I could, anywhere I could.

I was spending time with Spanish every day—and enjoying every second of it!

Little did I know, a lot of other things were also happening in the background as I made my way deeper and deeper into the Spanish language. For example, I only used free resources for English speakers instead of Greek speakers because there was a bigger variety, so my English also started to get better.

After three months of playing with Spanish online, I was looking for more free Spanish learning resources when I stumbled upon a language exchange meeting in my city: people scheduled a weekly meeting at a café to practice their foreign languages, including Spanish.

I had a strange thought: *What if I went out there and spoke Spanish?*

Me. Speaking Spanish. To others.

Suddenly, I was shivering with fear, remembering my horrible English-speaking experience with tourists in Chios. I remembered my terrible French. I recalled how miserably I failed in German. I couldn't let a horrible speaking experience spoil the fun I'd been having for three months now. Eventually, after much resistance, I changed my mind.

I went to the meeting.

There were two people speaking Spanish to each other. I was sweating all over—it was harder than I thought. But as I sat down and ordered a tea, my stress disappeared in an instant, and I started speaking Spanish. Words didn't come out easily at first, but I persisted. And suddenly, something unexpected happened.

People started complimenting me on my skills!

People were telling Maria that she was good at something!

How was that possible? All I did during those three months before the meeting was play with the language and discover things online to get to know more about it. I didn't think I was really learning the language; after all, I wasn't paying for a teacher or taking any courses. I didn't plan on taking any exams.

Despite all that, people commended I was good at Spanish. I'll never forget this day because it was the day everything started to change. I became more and more motivated to improve my Spanish and attended every one of those weekly meetings for the next three years. While it didn't always go smoothly and I made a lot of embarrassing mistakes along the way, I started changing from the inside out. I wasn't afraid of leaving my house anymore. In fact, I even made plans to travel outside the country alone for the first time.

I went to Spain to do volunteer work and felt like I was on a roller coaster. I was in another country, speaking a language that wasn't Greek or even English, and people complimented me on it *in Spain!*

That was an incredible feeling, and it made me question my whole mindset, my whole life up to that point. Where had *that kind* of language learning been all my life? All I did was spend a few minutes every day having fun with Spanish, and somehow it worked. I got better at it. I felt like I'd discovered a hidden treasure.

* * *

I haven't stopped learning languages. I've accomplished many, many things because of it (apart from learning seven languages), and it's changed me in ways I wouldn't have imagined.

- I overcame my panic attacks and insomnia.
- I started traveling abroad alone and moved to two different countries.
- I improved my self-discipline.
- I finished my studies, despite wanting to drop out of my university.
- I enhanced my sense of self-worth.

- I met fantastic people I'd otherwise never have met because they didn't speak Greek or English.
- People started asking me for advice on language learning—me!
- I was featured in an official schoolbook as a poster girl for effective language learning.
- I started doing radio and TV interviews.
- I made public speeches in front of hundreds of people, in languages other than my own.
- I worked for successful language learning websites.
- I realized I can actually cope with any difficulty that comes my way.

I learned to believe in myself and my powers. Before, I genuinely felt I couldn't be good at anything, even if others told me otherwise. I thought they were lying to make me feel good about myself. I presumed that whatever I'd achieved up to that point was because of pure luck.

Now I know that if I try to improve every day, if I have the hunger to become better, and if I have the will to move forward despite any obstacles that come my way, I can learn not only languages, but any other skill out there.

Who would have thought that something I detested would do so much for me?

My best friend even started complimenting me on how I opened up. "You were so shut off," he told me. "I had no idea what you were thinking, what you wanted. You're a different person now. And it's wonderful!"

That's why language learning has been the most wonderful accident I've ever had. What's more, it helped me achieve all these things for free, and I'm using everything I learned to write this book. I wasn't an author before, and English isn't my first language. Yet here I am, writing in English, because I felt an inner urge to help you embrace language learning and let it work its magic in your life.

I sincerely want it to change your life as much as it did mine, and I firmly believe it can do wonders for you. Despite any past failures you may have had, I urge you to reconsider learning a language. I ask you to trust in yourself, become the master of your language learning journey—and your life—and show everyone what you can do.

In this book, I'll assist you with doing all these things, and I'll enable you to eliminate any excuse that's holding you back—especially the one about not having enough money.

I'm sure the results will surprise you.

Are you ready?

Let's become fluent for free!

FLUENT FOR FREE? IS THIS FOR REAL?

Thanks to the Internet, it's absolutely possible to learn a language without spending a dime. We're blessed to live in this era where new information is only a click away. We don't have to go to libraries to search for a book to teach us what we want to know, running the risk that we won't find a book that suits our needs. And we certainly don't have to go to the country where our target language is spoken so that we can learn it. We browse the Internet every day to gather information about anything that interests us. Why not use it for language learning as well?

You see, the Internet is the *Place Where Our New Language Lives*, and that's how I'll refer to it throughout this book. If you want to learn a language without having to pay for it, then you have to leverage that magical place as often as possible. You have to take as many things as you can from it. You have to watch how this language lives, interacts, and of course, how it works.

But this isn't all it takes.

You have to change the way you approach a new language, the way you think you'll be able to learn it, and finally, the way you learn it. This will finally do the trick for you.

The secret lies in not only using and leveraging what the Internet has to offer, but also in changing your mindset so that you can make the most of your learning, thus ensuring that you will achieve your goals.

This is where this book serves as your guide.

WHO IS THIS BOOK FOR?

This book is for anyone who wants to learn a language effectively and for free. You don't have to have the language gene; you don't have to be smarter than average; you don't even have to have a lot of free time on your hands.

You're perfect for language learning, just the way you are. All you need are the desire to learn a language and an Internet connection, and you can make it happen. The changes you have to make are within your power; no external factors can prevent you from making them. If you learned how to speak, read, and write in your native language, then you can acquire any foreign language.

WHO IS THIS BOOK NOT FOR?

With that said, I have to make something clear from the beginning: if you're looking for a magic formula or a *perfect* method to learn a language with no effort—in two weeks, two months, or while you sleep—this book is *not* for you.

Language learning can't happen with the push of a button. If anyone promises you otherwise, then please run the other way as fast as you can.

Nothing worth having comes easy.

Think of the feelings you had when you achieved something that wasn't easy to do: winning a prize at a school competition, getting into the university you wanted, quitting a bad habit, doing better at a subject than someone you admire, overcoming a problem of any kind, or making a relationship work.

Now, reflect on the feelings you had when your parents bought you a new toy right after you asked for it, or when you found a movie after two minutes of looking for it on Netflix.

Those two sets of feelings are worlds apart, right?

You can't compare any feeling of instant gratification to your feeling of accomplishment when you've finally achieved something after a long time of trying and failing.

Think about the dreams you have. Maybe you dream of becoming successful, getting rich, becoming a master at a certain skill, or being loved. Are any of your dreams easy to accomplish? Allow me to assume otherwise.

The same idea applies to language learning. Part of what makes it worthwhile is that it's not easy to become fluent in a language. It takes time and effort. It's a journey with both ups and downs, with moments of embarrassment and failures, but also happiness and fulfillment. And in return, not only do you master a language, but you also get so much more!

Like I did.

The struggle is an asset, not a problem. There's true beauty in it!

Becoming fluent isn't as easy as listening to a language for three days and instantly sounding like a native speaker. But it isn't as hard as you think either.

HOW TO USE THIS BOOK

In this book I'll share with you the language learning methods that worked for me and which I continue to use to this day, and I also focus on what I call the "soft skills of language learning."

As you learn how to make the most out of the methods I suggest and how to combine them to create your personal learning plan and routine, you'll also notice I place a lot of emphasis on skills not directly connected with language learning.

There's a reason for that.

The majority of the books, courses, teachers and resources out there focus on the methods and the technical side of things, but not on these crucial skills that can make all the difference in your learning.

In reality, it's these soft skills that distinguish successful language learners from others who have tried learning a language but eventually quit. These soft skills are especially important, and once you've learned to use them, they'll make your learning a lot more effective, *even if you choose to use the exact methods you used before that didn't work.*

This book will serve as your step-by-step guide to changing your mentality, so that you can become a different person—a person capable of learning any language for free!

You'll take charge of your language learning journey, you'll set your personal goals and make sure you fulfill them, and you'll most definitely have fun!

You'll also find suggestions for learning languages that I've used throughout my journey that have worked for me, as well as fun tips and tricks for making the most out of any free method. I'll help you learn how to choose your own methods and style according to what suits you best and also how to solve common language learning problems. Finally, I'll help you maintain your motivation and discover how capable you are of teaching yourself any language.

Yes, learning for free means you won't need a teacher (unless you're able to convince one to teach you without charging you). I deeply admire language teachers and what they do, but if you want to become fluent for free, having a teacher isn't an option—and it doesn't have to be. What many successful language learners have in common is that we prefer teaching ourselves, so don't worry—we've got your back!

Armed with that new mentality ("I can do this, and I can have fun doing this!"), the soft skills, and the right method combination (which I'll show you how to design for yourself), you'll absolutely be able to learn a language successfully.

So sit back, relax, and discover what this book has to offer you. I recommend approaching the book in this order:

- Start by reading section 1, in which I teach you the first steps to take before you embark on a new language journey.
- Continue to section 2, which summarizes some of the free methods you can find out there.
- Go to section 3 next to determine which methods to choose from section 2 and how to fine-tune your language journey, so that everything works for you.
- Feel free to refer back to section 2 at any time if you feel like trying more methods.
- Whenever you feel frustrated or have problems of any kind, please refer to the "Troubleshooting" section where you'll locate the help and support you need. If you can't find the answer to your problem in that section, fear not. I've been through all kinds of language learning problems, so please feel free to contact me directly at maria@fluentforfree.com when all else fails.

But please, don't give up. That's not an option.

SECTION 1

Getting Started – Developing Your Mindset

"Miracles start to happen when you give as much energy to your dreams as you do to your fears."

—Buddha

WHAT'S STOPPING YOU? BUSTING COMMON LANGUAGE LEARNING MYTHS

Before we dive into the magical world of free language learning, I'd like to ask you to reflect on the obstacles that got in your way before and prevented you from learning the language of your dreams.

Was it because you couldn't afford it?

Was it because you felt you weren't good enough?

Was it based on a teacher who said you weren't capable of learning a language?

Spend the next few minutes and try to think of what exactly hasn't worked and why you haven't learned another language successfully so far.

Chances are, what stopped you from learning the language of your dreams was one of the common language learning myths we've all learned, which we keep using as excuses, even to ourselves.

To change your mentality toward language learning so that you can become successful at it, the first step you have to take is to unlearn these common language learning myths. Getting them out of your head (if you believe any of them) is crucial because—apart from the fact that they aren't true—they can seriously hinder your language learning abilities or even make you give up trying to learn a new language.

So let's have a look at the following myths and why they're false.

MYTH #1: I DON'T HAVE THE TALENT FOR LANGUAGE LEARNING

Whenever you hear someone speak a foreign language fluently, you can easily notice their skills, ease of saying things, speed, impeccable pronunciation, lack of hesitation, and lack of mistakes.

What you can't see (or hear) is the effort it took the speaker to reach that level, the hours put in, the mistakes made along the way, one's frustration, the times they couldn't articulate a single word, the occasions when one was on the brink of giving up, the actually quitting only to start again years later.

Instead, you assume that they became fluent easily, that someone just decided to learn a language and one's innate superpowers took care of the rest. You compare this person's skills to yours and offer reasons for that person's achievements and excuses for why you can't: *That person is so talented, and you're not. Unlike you, they never had moments of stress and frustration.*

I'm guilty of this, too. I used to think I didn't have the language gene. I regarded that others could do it, but I couldn't. I wasn't cut out for this, so why even bother trying?

Despite my lack of talent, I got into language learning, and a few years later, people started assuming I have an aptitude for languages.

Wait, what? Does that mean I acquired some kind of talent? Absolutely not.

Here's the truth: Our brains are wired to find the easiest way of doing things, a quick fix that can solve our problems and make us good at everything we want to do. Whenever we start something new, something out of the ordinary, our brains are the first to get in the way.

"Halt! Where do you think you're going?"

Did you hear that? It was your brain.

Simply put, our brains are the champions of self-sabotage. Once they realize there's no quick fix for language learning and fluency doesn't come overnight, they generate a ton of excuses to convince us we shouldn't even bother trying to learn, and we shouldn't feel bad about it because we lack something we can't possibly gain.

The master saboteur that is our brain wants us to retreat immediately to our comfort zone where things are nice and comfy, and it comes up with the most effective ways of doing that. If it didn't, what kind of champion would it be?

One phrase that our brain can always depend on to do the trick is—you guessed it—"I'm not talented enough to learn a language." You just need to recognize what your brain is trying to do when that self-defeating nonsense runs through your mind and ignore it.

Are you still not convinced? Then please consider this: if language learning really requires talent, how on earth does everybody learn one's first language? Let me try to answer this.

We learned our native language because:

- Our family exposed us to it every day.
- It took us a long time to start speaking it.
- When we did start speaking it, people corrected us every time we made mistakes.

- We were too young to care about what others thought of us, so we kept making mistakes and getting corrected.
- After some time, it stuck with us. Magic! Oh, la la!

So either we're all talented when it comes to learning languages, or—surprise, surprise—it doesn't require talent!

It's a myth that we need talent to learn a language. It's the champion (our brain) trying to sabotage us. While it's true that some people learn faster than others, fluency takes time and effort for all of us—even the gifted ones.

Hard work beats talent, and there are countless examples out there to prove that. This means that the actual difference between you and the fluent non-native speakers of your target language is that they found the courage to try learning the language and to work toward fluency, while you gave up on it (or didn't do much except talk or stress about it). Changing that mindset requires no talent. It requires *action*.

Fighting the champion isn't easy, but it *is* worth it. Ignore what your brain tells you and stick to language learning. Don't bring up talent again. If others can learn a foreign language, so can you!

MYTH #2: I DON'T HAVE TIME TO LEARN A LANGUAGE!

Sometimes life gets in the way. We're all busy people, and as time passes and the pace of life gets faster and faster, we become busier and busier. We're always present in our jobs because of technology, and we're commuting to work and back home, taking care of the kids, going to the university, studying, … the list is endless, isn't it? How can we ever fit language learning into our busy schedules? Doesn't it take too much time?

The truth is that it doesn't have to take much time. Successful language learners and polyglots have proven that studying more often is more effective than studying longer. In fact, I'd go so far as to say that thirty minutes a day is all you need to successfully learn a language. No matter how busy your schedule is, you can most definitely set aside half an hour, either first thing in the morning or right before bed.

You could also make use of the time you spend waiting for the bus or the train, waiting for a lecture, or having your lunch break at work. I've discovered that there's a lot of "dead time" during the day that can be used for learning. I learned Spanish by using the time I spent on public transport and then a couple minutes before I went to bed.

If you don't have time, *make time!*

MYTH #3: I'M TOO OLD TO LEARN A LANGUAGE!

I've heard this complaint way too many times.

"Oh, of course you can learn languages easily. You're so young—you're in your twenties! If I were your age and wanted to learn languages, I would've pulled it off, too. But now it's simply too late. I'm too old for that; and as people get older, it gets increasingly hard for them to learn new things, let alone remember words in a foreign language!"

After watching famous middle-aged or older polyglots make it work (as well as my own aunt and father, who are both in their sixties), I can proudly say none of this is true.

After a lifetime of speaking only his native Greek, at the age of sixty-three, my father decided to start learning German. In less than a year of learning it on his own, for free, he's improved a lot. He even came to Germany to visit me, and I let him do all the talking and solve any problems using only German. He succeeded in all of it.

At the age of seventy-six, the previously monolingual grandfather of a friend of mine decided to learn French on his own. Now, at the age of seventy-nine, he not only speaks it fluently, but he also speaks it with a great accent, as a French friend of mine told me as soon as she heard him speak. That's not something you'd expect from someone his age who spent a lifetime being monolingual, is it?!

If you need further convincing, check out Steve Kaufmann, a famous polyglot who speaks sixteen languages, has studied a dozen more, and is in his late fifties. He's very active on the web as he runs his own website, LingQ, and he has a YouTube channel.

So no, old age isn't an obstacle for language learning. On the contrary, being older can actually be an asset to language learning!

If you're a pensioner (retired), you have so much more time on your hands that you can use to learn languages than students or people of working age have. My father takes advantage of this fact, which is how he's able to make so much progress in so little time!

As we previously discussed, you always have time for language learning, but if you learn smart and dedicate more time to it, you'll definitely see better results. So instead of using "old age" as an excuse, use it to your advantage.

MYTH #4: I'M TOO SHY TO LEARN A LANGUAGE!

I'm very familiar with this excuse. I used to use it a lot since I was (and still am) quite shy and try to avoid human interaction as much as possible, let alone interact in a language other than my own!

It's no surprise, then, that during my first six years of learning, I avoided talking to native speakers. Yet I learned quite a few languages! Did I stop being shy to pull it off? No! I just decided to turn that weakness of mine into a strength and use it to my advantage instead of as an obstacle between me and my target language.

I thought every public use of my target language would be an exam, and I'd be judged harshly for that. The mere thought of uttering a single word in a foreign language always made my heart race. In fact, when I traveled to a country where my target language was spoken, I did everything in my power to evade talking to locals. I even avoided asking for crucial instructions on how to find my way in the cities! I spent years dodging interactions with native speakers, but everything wasn't gloomy for me.

Even though I was trying to avoid native speakers, I still wanted to learn languages, so I chose to speak to fellow learners and only in language cafes and groups of people. That way, I wouldn't be the center of attention, and at the same time I'd only have to say a phrase or two in my target language. I limited myself because of my shyness, but at the same time I challenged myself to get out of my comfort zone and keep learning *despite* being shy.

I'd always limited myself this way, but I didn't want to believe that getting over my shyness was the *only* way to learn languages. After all, I was in love with all my languages. I'd even say a phrase or two to fellow learners and feel extremely accomplished because of that.

I decided, why give all that up just because I'm shy?

In Section 2, you'll find some methods that you can use (without any problems) as a shy introvert and become better in your new language.

MYTH #5: TO LEARN A LANGUAGE, I HAVE TO TRAVEL TO THE COUNTRY WHERE IT'S SPOKEN.

Fortunately, no, you don't.

Traveling to the country where your target language is spoken may be a boost for your motivation to become better at the language, but you don't have to do that to actually learn it. I've acquired most of my languages while living in my home country.

Don't forget that the countries where your new language is spoken are not the only places where it lives. The Internet is the Place Where Your New Language Lives! It's forever changed the way people learn languages, and it's patiently waiting for you to make use of it—right here, right now. You can learn any language from the comfort of your own home!

MYTH #6: SUCCESSFUL LANGUAGE LEARNERS AND POLYGLOTS SPEND TOO MUCH TIME STUDYING.

Most polyglots and successful language learners will happily confirm that all it takes is studying every day, no matter how long. All you have to do is create a chain and make sure you don't break it (Even if you pause for a day or two, or even a week, make sure you jump back in and get back to studying every day.) Half an hour—heck, even fifteen minutes—is enough. Do this for a week and pay attention to how much you improved by dedicating just fifteen minutes a day to learning your target language.

You absolutely don't have to study long hours to learn a language, unless you're obsessed with it or want to learn it as soon as possible. But even then, studying smart and as often as you can is more effective than spending long hours studying in a way that doesn't really work for you and that makes the whole language learning process a chore.

MYTH #7: LANGUAGE LEARNING IS EXPENSIVE!

No, it absolutely is not. This is what this book is all about! Let me repeat this:

If you have an Internet connection, you don't have to pay for language learning.

As previously reiterated, the Internet has forever changed the way we learn languages, and it's become a Place Where All Languages Live. I've used it to learn languages for free. If I can do it, so can you!

MYTH #8: I'M NOT SMART ENOUGH TO LEARN A LANGUAGE!

This is something I expressed too many times before. It's a common myth that learning foreign languages requires above-average intelligence. But is it true?

How many times have you encountered someone that you know is of lower than average intelligence? But given that, haven't they all learned their native language? How were they able to do that?

Maybe you're thinking that we learn our native language differently. We learn it when we're kids, when our brains are like sponges, so it's a different situation. We're not deliberately trying to shove a new language into our brains; instead, we're exposed to it, and we gradually learn. Let's suppose you're right and learning our own language is an exception.

That brings us back to the original question: if we're to learn another language, we have to be very intelligent, right?

Well, not quite. First of all, I can speak many languages, but I assure you I'm no smarter than average. I've also known quite a few people with below-average intelligence who have learned another language. For instance, a few years ago, when I spoke only Greek and some English, I came across an acquaintance who was speaking fluent Italian. I caught myself wondering, "How on earth did this *stupid guy* learn that language so well?"

It baffled me. I thought the gift of language learning was reserved for the talented and clever, but that man didn't fall into either of those categories—yet he spoke Italian fluently. What kind of sorcery was this?

It was years later when it occurred to me to ask myself a simple question: *If this stupid guy is able to learn another language, why can't I do the same?*

Unknowingly, I took that example and used it to my advantage. I encourage you to do the same: try to use everything that comes your way to your advantage.

MYTH #9: THERE'S A PERFECT METHOD FOR EVERYONE!

This myth is deeply ingrained in our minds and pops up often as we search for that magic formula to learn a language effortlessly and at lightning speed. I used to believe this, too. To be honest, it was even worse for me because I thought there was a perfect method to learn a language in the classroom, *but it didn't work for me because I wasn't good enough.*

If you've scanned the Internet, you've seen that it offers methods that not only work perfectly for everyone, but they also require little effort and promise language proficiency in a matter of months—or even weeks!

We buy into such claims because we strive for a fast solution to our problems. We want something done quickly with the least amount of effort, so we want to believe such methods exist and that they do as they promise.

Sorry to burst your bubble, but there's *no* such method out there!

Why? Because every one of us is different.

Teachers use methods that have been proven to work for many people, but there are people like me who still find classroom language learning boring and for whom these methods don't work. I can't get myself to concentrate during private classes either, even though I've tried this method, too. So why do classroom language learning and private lessons with a great teacher work for others, but not for people like me?

Not everyone learns the same way, which I discovered after months of teaching myself my first foreign language, Spanish.

With all of this said, please allow me to correct the title of this myth so that it's no longer a myth but a statement of fact:

THERE'S *AN EFFECTIVE COMBINATION OF METHODS FOR YOU* TO LEARN A LANGUAGE *FOR THE TIME BEING*.

Successful language learners and polyglots may swear that there's a perfect method that they use that enables them to learn effectively and fast. And you know what? They'd be absolutely right if they added these two words: "These methods are perfect *for me.*" Those methods work for them, and *maybe* they'll work for you too. But don't take their word for it because there's not one perfect method out there that can take you from absolute beginner to completely fluent.

There is, however, a certain mindset that enables you to find *your favorite set of methods*. Once you adopt this mindset, it'll be just a matter of time before you find the most suitable methods for you.

Now I want you to notice that I also added "for the time being" to my newly titled, no-longer-a-myth statement of fact. After seven years of teaching myself languages, I've found that I don't always use the same methods. Specifically, I used a different set of methods to learn each of my seven foreign languages because each language is different, and, well, I was also changing as a person. I even used different methods throughout the course of learning just one language.

So don't be afraid to try different methods and change what you don't like. If you're struggling, that doesn't mean you can't learn your language; it means you haven't found your favorite set of methods yet. I'll show you exactly how to choose your methods and when to change methods in Section 3.

But why do you need to look for *a set* of methods? Why not just one method? Isn't one enough?

No method is perfect, which is why using a combination of methods is much more effective than following just one. If you choose just one method, there might be gaps that method doesn't really cover that you nevertheless want to fill. You can do so by using a supplementary method. Also, if one method takes too much time and you're really busy, you can supplement it with another, faster method you can follow anywhere and that you can use even during small increments of time. Confused? No worries, we'll look at that in more detail in Section 3.

Now that we've debunked these myths, it's important that you stop believing them before you embark on a language journey. Put those myths behind you, and let's move on to see what's next.

SETTING YOUR FLUENCY FOUNDATIONS

With those myths dispelled and behind us, there are two basic questions to ask yourself before starting your language learning journey. Take some time to ponder your answers and then write them down.

START WITH WHY

The first question you should ask yourself is *why* you want to learn your target language. This might seem obvious, but it's crucial not to overlook it and to answer it early on.

Take a moment of silence to think of the answer. As you do this, perhaps more and more reasons will emerge? We want this to happen. You see, there are different *whys*, and you have to find the one that *speaks* to you the most. Answering this question is not as simple as it seems; it's a process, and if you find your personal reasons, you'll become even more motivated.

Let me give you an example.

I wanted to learn German, but I didn't think about *why* I wanted to learn the language because to me it was obvious: I wanted to learn to speak German to help me with my career as an engineer.

I tried again and again to learn German, but I failed over and over again. I lost motivation fast, and I gave up on learning German three times.

Now, though, I can speak it, and I live in Germany!

What happened? What made me finally get serious about German and take that step to become fluent in it?

The turning point was I finally answered that *why* question, and I found that the reason I wanted to learn German wasn't really *mine*. My *why* was coming from sources outside me, sources that were dictating that I should learn it because a European mechanical engineer without German misses a lot of what's out there, including job opportunities.

That reason made perfect sense. I knew I had to do it because it would help me. But the problem was that this *why* wasn't coming from *me*. It was someone else's.

My journey with German finally worked as soon as I found *my own reason* to study it.

Before I took up German for the fourth time, I got very excited about European history, especially the Cold War. I started reading what life was like for people on both sides of the Iron Curtain and how everything led to the events of 1989.

The focal point of the Cold War in Europe was Germany, which was split into two different countries at that time. I'd read almost everything I could find in English, and then I hit a barrier. I wanted to learn from Germans themselves what their lives were like—Germans that lived and experienced that era firsthand, especially the 1980s. The problem was that they all spoke about it in German to each other! And while there were quite a few resources in English, my lack of skills in German hindered my ability to get into those people's heads and understand what was going on from their own perspective. In the meantime, I also discovered music and movies from that era, and of course, everything was in German.

So my *hunger* to know more about that time was the real reason *why* I wanted to learn German. No one had instructed me to study what was going on in Germany in the '80s; *I* was the one who wanted to do that. No one had told me to watch movies and enjoy the music of that era; *I* chose to do it. Finally, the reason *why* I wanted to learn German was 100 percent mine, and that's what made me finally succeed in it.

As I dove deeper into the language, I also fell in love with the way it sounded. I enjoyed listening to myself trying to imitate this beautiful language (which came later!). Sometimes you have to really get involved with something to experience it fully and finally fall in love with it.

Another example is my *why* for learning Basque.

Whenever people asked me why I was learning the Basque language, I'd answer, "Because it's different, non-Indo-European. Because it's beautiful and mysterious. No one knows how old it is or where it comes from, and it also sounds absolutely great. I fell in love with it as soon as I heard it for the first time."

These reasons are all true, and I still believe each and every one of them. But they weren't *my* reasons to learn Basque. My real rationale was that I fell in love with someone whose mother tongue was Basque, and I wanted to learn the language to impress them.

That personal *why* was powerful enough to get me going and learn that language, and it held everything together when I was extremely frustrated. Even though my plan for us to be together never worked, I still speak the language, and I gained so much more because of that. In fact, I'd argue that of all the languages I speak, Basque has given me the most so far, with German being a close second.

So please, take some time (five to ten minutes) and jot down all the reasons—all your *whys*—you want to learn your target language. As soon as you find one that speaks to you the most and even makes you emotional, stop. This is your number one reason *why* you want to learn that language (If it has to do with finding a better job, then great; just make sure it's coming from *you*, not the people around you).

Write your *why* on a piece of paper and hang it on your bedroom wall so that you can see it all the time, especially when you feel demotivated and want to give up. It'll further remind you *why* you do what you do, *why* it's worth it to keep going, despite those pesky irregular verbs or a failed speaking experience.

NEXT QUESTION: HOW COULD I MAKE IT FUN?

I used to ask myself, why does language learning have to be boring? Why does it require boring texts, boring exercises, stress, and endless tests? Where does *fun* fit in? Why do school systems repeatedly ignore the *fun*?

Having fun is by far the best motivator when it comes to learning languages. Only when you really enjoy something do you want to do it repeatedly, day after day. Consider the following ways we can flip the script:

Why follow a textbook, when you can read and study your favorite novel (or narrative nonfiction) in your target language?

Why listen to recorded dialogues of people having dull conversations, when you can watch your favorite movie in your target language, listening to the dialogues and maybe even using subtitles?

Why do boring written exercises, when you can play your favorite online game, choose a server in the country where your target language is spoken, and practice it with fellow gamers?

Why take speaking tests, when you can find interesting people for chatting in your target language?

Anything you do in your own language, you can do in your target language—for example, your favorite hobbies and activities. Why not watch an instructional video on how to improve your cooking skills in your target language? Why not view an important basketball match online in your target language? Why not meditate in your target language? Instructors always speak slowly in a calm, soothing voice, so you can concentrate on the language and its sounds, thus improving your listening and vocabulary skills.

If you turn to fun activities instead of boring ones, your resentment will gradually turn into enthusiasm, and you'll be excited and eager to start learning your target language—which means you'll keep doing it every day and great results will come, guaranteed.

So your second question is: how can I make language learning fun?

You don't have to come up with an exact plan right now. Just think about everything you enjoy doing because you might be able to combine those things with language learning!

To recap, the two questions you need to have in mind before you start are "What's my *why*?" and "How can I make this fun?" Now let's see what it takes to learn a language.

If you get started and find yourself frustrated and feeling like it's too much work, you might think that it would be simpler to just hire a teacher. They could do the job for you, right?

This is a big mistake most language learners make, and I used to make it a lot, too. That's why, before I taught myself Spanish, I failed every time I tried to learn a language.

We expect teachers or language courses to do the work for us. These people are experts; and as experts they must be powerful enough to shove the language into our brains and make us fluent without any effort from us, right here, right now.

That's not possible, and that's not why teachers do what they do.

A language teacher's job is to show you what you should learn and how you should learn it. Teachers don't teach you languages. They teach you how to learn languages. There's a difference. They help you learn a language. *You* must do the work!

Once you realize what teachers are there to do for you, you can take over and do their job for free instead.

You might not be that experienced, you might not know what language resources to use, it might take you a long time to figure out what works best for you, but hey, you know yourself best. You know what you want, what you like, and what you find boring. Language teachers may know how to teach languages better than you, but they don't know you better than you know yourself.

So try to be your own leader and see how it goes. I did, and I've never looked back. Even here in Germany, I didn't take any German language courses, although some of them were very cheap and I could have afforded them if I'd wanted to try them. Thankfully, when I arrived, my German was already decent, so nobody ever proposed that I take any.

The point is, once you learn how to become your own teacher, how to organize and plan your learning journey in detail, and how to have fun in the process, you'll never want to have a language teacher again. And the more languages you learn, the more experienced you'll become regarding what to acquire and how to learn it. That's what many polyglots do, and I'm proposing a free version of this in my book.

If you manage to do the teacher's job for yourself, you won't have to pay a teacher. If you succeed in creating language learning material out of anything you can find out there, you won't have to pay for language learning ever again.

Become the leader of your journey, and you won't have to pay for a language teacher again.

Create your own language learning material, and you won't have to pay for language learning again.

Excited? Ready to try this out and become your own teacher? Read on!

BREAKING DOWN LANGUAGES

Let's get down to the meaty part now. If you try to analyze a foreign language in a practical way, you'll see that all languages consist of the following:

- Vocabulary
- Grammar
- Pronunciation (and Alphabet)

The vital organs of each language include its vocabulary (the words that make it up). When we listen to a language being spoken, we hear a series of different words put together to convey a certain message.

Grammar represents the backbone of the language, the skeleton that makes sure the vital organs are secure and in place. Without the skeleton, the vital organs have no structure.

Pronunciation and alphabet are the cells, which comprise the skeleton *and* the vital organs. Without them, there's nothing. There's no language.

Learning the alphabet is optional. If you're already familiar with the alphabet of the language you're studying, that's great, but regardless, you have to pay attention to the different sounds the letters may represent in the new language.

So to expand upon former learning, when we hear a language, we hear a series of different sounds put together for the sake of communication. Vocabulary, grammar, and pronunciation-alphabet are what I call the **Key Ingredients of a Language**.

Of course, the following *language skills* are also applicable:

- Reading
- Listening
- Speaking
- Writing

But if we were to break down these skills, we'd go back to our three core ingredients of a language.

- Reading means looking at *grammar, alphabet, and vocabulary.*
- Listening involves hearing *pronunciation, vocabulary, and grammar.*
- Writing refers to producing *grammar, alphabet, and vocabulary.*
- Speaking reflects the creation of *grammar, vocabulary, and pronunciation.*

This means that whatever skill you want to focus on, you have to work on the three key ingredients. If you feel you're not good at listening or speaking, focus on the key ingredients of each skill. That's where you'll find what's missing.

Let's say you experience problems with understanding people. You feel like your listening skills aren't good enough and you need to improve. Essentially, you can improve them by listening to the language. Exposing yourself more and more to the sounds of it, so that they become second nature will help you to finally comprehend what's going on.

But that's not enough.

If you don't expand your vocabulary or learn how words are pronounced, you might get used to the sounds of the language, but you'll reach a line you won't be able to cross and will have difficulties understanding most of what you hear. We'll see exactly how you can improve your listening skills in the "Listening" chapter in section 2.

If you have no problem with vocabulary but you struggle with grammar and pronunciation, then listening becomes easier because you can deduce what the person is talking about from the words you understand. However, speaking is harder, so again, think of the key ingredients. It's highly likely that you'll solve your speaking problem by improving at least one of them.

Now I want you to consider which skills you want to improve in your target language and why you want to do so. It's time to set your own learning goals!

SETTING LANGUAGE LEARNING GOALS

Now that you've figured out your personal "why" for learning a language, let's look at it in practice. What exactly do you want to achieve?

According to many language schools, textbooks, and courses out there (who think they know your personal language learning goals), you should obviously want to learn how to book hotels in your target language or learn all the colors in the language. The reality is, you'll most likely book hotels online in your own language, and you probably won't be choosing curtain colors in your target language (at least not early on—and apologies if that's your goal). No. You're the leader of your language learning journey, and you decide what your personal goals are when it comes to learning the language.

Remember: You're the one trying to make a foreign language your own. No one knows your language goals better than you do.

So what do you want to achieve in the new language?

You might be tempted to answer, "I want to speak fluently." But what does "speak fluently" really mean? Isn't it ambiguous? Do you want to be able to speak about everything, make no mistakes whatsoever, know all the words there are in the language, and never, ever hesitate?

If that's what fluency is to you, then I have a question for you: can you do all of that in your native language?

No? But you're fluent in your native language, aren't you?

My point is that it's time we define what fluency really is. Greek is my native language, yet I still learn new words from time to time and even make minor mistakes. What's going on? Am I not fluent in Greek? Is it reasonable for me to expect that I'll be able to speak about everything, make no mistakes, comprehend all the words in a new language and never hesitate when speaking it when I can't even do that in my own language—the language I grew up with?

It's time to replace that vague "fluent" with something more concrete, more particular, more personal. For example:

I want my German to be better than any other foreign languages I speak.

That's what I normally say whenever somebody asks me what I want to achieve in German, but this goal is still not concrete enough. What does "better" mean? As good as my native Greek? Better than the other foreign languages I speak, but still not as good as Greek? And in what way is it going to be better?

It's getting really complicated. Let's break that vague goal into smaller, more concrete goals:

I want to be able to understand and speak about engineering in German without hesitation because it's what I studied at the university, and I'd love to work as an engineer in Germany. I want to be able to achieve this by June this year.

Now that's a concrete goal. It tells me I should concentrate on vocabulary that has to do with engineering, watch engineering videos in German, talk to engineers, visit engineering sites, and read engineering books in German in the library. I also have a realistic deadline, so I know that if I keep at it regularly, it's doable. Notice the difference between this and the prior goal of simply being "better" in German?

When you set a concrete goal, you automatically know what to learn, what you should concentrate on, and where to start.

Another example of a concrete goal would be:

I also want to be able to understand and communicate freely with people who work at my bank, staff in the shops where I visit, and my landlord. I want this to happen by January.

With this concrete goal, I now know I should concentrate on banking-related vocabulary, all parts of the house, and everything about the services I regularly use.

I could have simply said, "I want to get by in Germany." That's way easier and faster to say than talking about shops and banks, but it offers no direction for what I should learn and what I should focus on. *Getting by*... What does that mean in practice?

These goals don't have to be universal and last forever. They can be small goals (like this one) so that they get you started and you create a plan. You'll fulfill them more easily than the "becoming fluent" one, and you'll be able to celebrate your small victory and get the boost to keep learning and setting new goals.

Other examples of goals may be:

I want to read the history of China from Chinese sources by 2021 because I have to spend a year in China as a history researcher.

I want to write articles and blog posts about beauty and wellness in English by September this year because I want to set up an English blog on those topics.

My husband is Guatemalan, so I want to be able to have basic conversations about everyday topics with him by August.

You want to make sure you have a deadline—a realistic one so you won't get frustrated if you don't succeed—and that you know where to start, that you have something specific in mind that you want to fulfill.

The goal could be even smaller and last for a shorter time. For example:

I want to have my first conversation in Japanese with a native speaker by next month.

That conversation could be as simple as introducing yourself and talking to a native speaker about basic topics for fifteen minutes. It doesn't matter how long you talk or what you talk about; all that matters is that your goal gets you started, and that you know what to learn, what you want to achieve, and how you'll do it.

Achieving that goal means you got out of your comfort zone and will have started actually speaking in the language! After that, those fifteen minutes can become thirty, and the conversation with a native speaker can become a weekly (or even daily) activity. You might then change your mind and focus on writing instead, and choose a goal like the following:

Write a fifty-word paragraph in Japanese by May this year

The content of your goal doesn't matter. As long as you know what you want to achieve and by what time you want to master it, everything will be a lot easier for you.

Are you ready to set your goals?

Put the book down and spend five to ten minutes thinking about your current language learning goals (big or small). Next, grab a piece of paper and write them all down. Then select one or two and focus on them first. Post them somewhere that you can see them first thing in the morning.

If you're not much of a planner and prefer to rely on your *why* to learn a language, that's perfectly okay. Spending time learning is always more valuable than spending time planning. You can just focus on enjoying the process of learning, or you can come up with very short-term, easily achievable goals.

So while setting goals can help you progress faster in the exact direction you want to go, you can learn a new language without having any goals, other than your personal *why*. In the next chapter, however, I'm going to share with you something that's essential to a successful learning journey.

TRAIN YOUR BRAIN - A NEW MENTALITY

As we previously discussed, having the right mentality is key. It's what distinguishes successful from unsuccessful language learning. Yes, the *mindset* matters more than the methods or the hours applied.

If you can:

- Choose learning methods that are fun and effective for you
- Create a study routine according to your *why* or your goals
- Learn every day and expose yourself to your new language as often as possible

Then you can master any language successfully.

All successful language learners and polyglots have this in common. They know their *why* (which sometimes makes them obsessed with the language—and that helps a lot), they use (or create) their favorite methods and language material, enjoy what they do, and learn every day, even spending even as little as fifteen minutes a day.

These tips make all the difference. It's not *just* the methods they follow.

NECESSITY STIMULATES CREATIVITY

Necessity is the mother of invention; there's no denying that.

If you go to a poor neighborhood in any city and examine the houses closely, you'll see a lot of amazing, very creative inventions people have formulated, so that they can get what they want despite not having the money to pay for it—from housing foundations and painting styles to creating their own satellite dishes and protection from the rain for their roofs.

Necessity stimulates creativity and drives people forward.

In this case, you need to learn a foreign language successfully and find 100 percent free materials you can use to work your way to fluency. When you can't locate a free language course, you have two options: pay for a paid course or create your own personalized course.

When you can't find a teacher to ask a language-related question that's been bothering you, you have two options: pay for a language teacher or google your way to the answer for free.

Whenever a free version of an app expires, you have two options: pay for the paid version or devise with a way to create or use something similar to that app.

You may think that the second option in these examples would require too much time and effort, but in fact it can lead to greater things than instantly gratifying your desires. These options teach you how to find 100 percent personalized material, how to find exactly what you're looking for, and even how to remember a new concept more easily in the language because you actually had to google it.

By choosing to learn for free, you're actually creating an environment that stimulates creativity and innovation. You know what your limits are, yet you choose to work around them accordingly.

That's what makes people grow.

In essence, I have numerous stories I could share about how I learned very important things in my new languages as I was looking for something else. Even if I didn't find the exact answer to my initial question, I'd find so much more by just taking action and actively looking for what I wanted. I'd locate interesting material to jot down in my notebook so that I could learn, and I'd end up asking the question somewhere online and have it answered.

So by taking the hard, seemingly more time-consuming road (the *free* way), I ended up learning *so much more*. I'd ultimately jot down four or five new phrases to learn instead of just the one I was looking for initially.

You can learn *so much* in your new language *just by googling one phrase in it!*

If you do this, you'll create your own language learning material for days to come. You could discover new phrases to master (therefore new vocabulary and grammar), a new grammar rule you heard a native speaker use somewhere in the Place Where Your New Language Lives, a new language-related forum where people ask questions about the languages they're studying and get answers, or a cool new site in your new language that you can visit again and again whenever you want!

All I did was use Google when I had to deal with limited learning resources for not-so-popular languages. It's tempting to ask whether you can actually google your way into *any* language if languages are rare and have few to no resources. Try it and see what (or who) you can find! It's highly likely that there are specialized websites for these languages.

As we previously discussed, though, free language learning is so much more than just using Google. Let's find out what other free methods you can use to collect your materials and improve any language skills you want without breaking the bank.

SECTION 2

Free Methods and Resources

"Learning is a treasure that will follow its owner everywhere."

—Chinese proverb

In this section of the book, we'll explore how to collect existing language learning materials, what free methods are out there, and how to make our own language learning resources.

Up to now, you've probably never collected language material by yourself and it might sound foreign to you since your teachers and textbooks used to do it for you. We've already talked about how they know better, right?

The thing is, each and every one of us is different, and although foreign languages have the same words, the same grammar, the same sounds, and the same rules for everyone, why should we all learn the same things, read the same texts (even if they are of absolutely no interest to us), use the same textbooks, and memorize the same words? Is this a proven way to become fluent in the language faster or more effectively? If so, why have so many of us (myself included) taken years of language classes but still can't use the language?

That's exactly why learning how to collect material according to your own personal needs is important, and it's also what a lot of successful language learners do. They don't expect any teacher to do the work for them. They critically think about how to learn a language themselves and experiment with methods to see if they work for them.

You're the leader of your language journey, so you're the one who chooses what to learn. But how can you do this in practice?

By using the Place Where All Languages Live—the Internet!

Note: I will mention some websites and apps in this section. You can find links to these pages and apps at fluentforfree.com/links.

COLLECTING MATERIAL ON THE INTERNET - CRITERIA AND APPROACHES

If you google "how to learn X language for free" (where X is your target language), you'll surely find numerous sites out there promising to teach you that language. If it's a platform promising to teach you that language for free, you can choose that and use it until you become fluent. If it's a free language course, you can use it instead, and that's it.

Many people do this, but sadly they stop there. Even if they manage to follow everything and reach a conversational level in the language using these sites, they feel they have to turn to traditional ways of learning a language to advance further in their target language. So they start looking for teachers, special courses for intermediate learners, or language classes.

The reality is, the free language learning material available online doesn't stop there.

It's everywhere.

Think of the reasons—all the reasons—you use the internet. They could range from getting informed about current events (or anything that interests you) and talking to your friends to wanting Google to give you an opinion on how to choose clothes, how to repair something in your house, or how to speak in public, for example. You do all that in your native language.

Practically, other people use the Internet—in their own languages—for the same reasons. And you can find what they're talking about, what pages they visit, where they get their information, and where they ask questions. Catch my drift?

You can use the Internet to figure out how people live in your target language. The potential language learning material there is endless. They talk to their friends, ask questions, get informed about fixing cars, researching parenting strategies, playing basketball, cooking interesting recipes, solving mental problems and insecurities, politics, astronomy—anything. And all that information is available to you.

The Internet is full of opportunities. Every website you enter that is in your target language is language learning material, even if it was built for native speakers. Try finding a site that's in your target language, see what phrases you can find and use, note them down, and learn them. It's all there for you; you just have to spot it, take it, and use it!

In this way, you can find out how real people speak your target language on a daily basis, not how books tell you it should be spoken. People tend to write exactly how they speak, and you can read comments, blog posts, diary entries, and essays, to name just a few. You can see what words and phrases people actually use, so that if you know two words that mean the same thing, you can choose the right one—the one a native speaker would choose.

As long as you start looking at the Internet as your source for endless language learning material, you can use it to improve your language skills, no matter what your current level in the language is, even if you're at an upper-intermediate level and want to become fluent.

True, people might make mistakes or misspell words in their own language, but there are ways to check whether what you've found and want to learn is correct. A lot of languages have their own place where people ask questions about them. For example, German has its own bilingual question and answer site, Stack Exchange, and Spanish and other languages have Wordreference forums. There's also a tiny, beautiful Android and iOS app called "HiNative" that enables you to ask native speakers of your target language anything you don't understand about the language—whether a phrase sounds natural, whether or not they would use it, and whether something you found is correct, for example.

Think about that: there are hidden teachers out there you can access for free. There are people eager to help you learn their language in any way, for free. All you have to do is look for them and ask for their help.

If you happen to live in the country where your target language is spoken, then you can find free language learning material everywhere, even if you just pay attention to what people are talking about on the bus. You can grab a notebook, and as you listen, jot down phrases you hear and—boom! You have authentic language learning materials (Just try not to be too obvious because they might think you're a spy or something)!

Collecting language learning materials can be as simple as gathering phrases of interest online and offline and jotting them down in your notebook (In case you haven't noticed, I think it's a great idea to have a notebook (traditional or digital) just for your target language, so that you can record phrases and words you want to learn there).

You might be thinking that you'll be working 24/7 just to write down everything, but you don't have to learn everything you hear or see, of course. Here are some criteria to choose phrases to learn from your notebook or to collect language learning material online.

- Relevance: What do you want to learn first? What's more relevant to you? What interests you the most—your job and hobbies or how to explain the rules of golf to a foreigner, for example? You decide.

- **Usage:** What am I highly likely to use as soon as I strike up a conversation with a native speaker, write my diary entry in the language, talk about myself, or achieve any other goal in the language?
- **Necessity:** What do I have to talk about now? For example, if you live in a country where your target language is spoken and you have to call your Internet provider to let them know something's wrong with your Internet connection, you might want to learn some Internet-related vocabulary to use immediately. How would you say "I've had connection problems since yesterday" in your target language? You may have to use that on the phone!
- **Conversation topic:** What are you going to talk about with your conversational partner? Let's say you've scheduled a conversation with a native speaker of your target language, and you've agreed on the topic. Or let's imagine you're joining a language exchange meeting and they've agreed on a specific topic. You'll want to collect material relevant to that topic, learn it, prepare scripts with it, and use it.
- **Exams:** Let's envision you want to take a test in your target language. You'll naturally want to collect material that helps you pass the exams—or even practice tests to see what they want from you so that you can ace those exams. I've used these criteria to prepare for language-related exams since I always learn alone and have no teachers to do that job for me. It sounds risky, but I have a 100 percent success rate in language tests so far, so I know it works (more on that later).
- **Playfulness:** If you just want to play with the language to become more familiar with it, you can search for websites or platforms where you can start learning a language by doing simple, fun exercises.
- **Teach me, Master:** You look for free online courses and choose to follow the ones you like the most. That way, even though the courses tell you what you should learn, you chose the courses, so

you're still the leader of your language journey. You can follow one or two courses, and as soon as you finish them, you'll have some basic knowledge in the language.

Notes: There's no either/or here. You can use all the criteria at once. If you find an online platform to play with the language, you can skip some sentences and learn others. That way you both play with the language and learn by relevance and necessity. It's up to you!

Also, you don't have to collect all the necessary language learning materials before you start learning the language. This is a gradual process that has to happen during your journey. It's something you can do for just a little bit every day.

If that sounds too demanding or time-consuming for you, don't worry. After you've done this once or twice, you'll get used to it and it will become second nature. For example, you can start by collecting just five phrases that you want to learn today, and then write them in an online post or use them to talk to people—all in one day. It's not a serial procedure; you just collect new phrases at will.

Let's look at an example of collecting materials in practice.

Think about an answer to this question: what would you like to learn how to say in the language right now?

"What kind of question is that?" you might be thinking. "Of course I want to learn everything."

Sure, but let's start somewhere.

I always ask myself that question when I'm learning a new language, and most of the time I answer, "I'd like to learn how to introduce myself."

Your answer depends on what you want to say. If the very first phrase you want to learn is, "My hovercraft is full of eels," then by all means go for it.

But let's say you want to learn how to introduce yourself. Now what?

Try googling "basic phrases in X language," where X is your target language.

Let's ponder you land on a page with ten basic phrases in your target language. If you're coming from a traditional language class background, your first thought is probably that you have to memorize all these phrases, as if it were another textbook.

But it's not a textbook, and let's not forget that you're the leader of your journey. You wanted to learn how to introduce yourself, so all you need to do is choose the phrases that you would use for that.

For example, if there are phrases in your target language for:

"Hello!"

"My name is X."

"I don't understand."

"I want to book a hotel."

"Where's the train station?"

"I'm learning the Y language."

Instead of learning all the phrases at once, stick to your plan and choose the phrases "Hello!" "My name is X," and "I am learning the Y language" because that's your goal right now.

Now you might argue that we're just using "canned phrases" instead of breaking down each word and discovering the grammar rules behind it and what each word means, to which I'd reply, that's true. If you want to learn those elements, you can totally do that instead. This was just an example of collecting material using the "Necessity" criteria.

Now let's move on to the methods and materials that are out there.

We've already talked about the Key Ingredients of a Language (vocabulary, grammar, pronunciation) as well as the language skills (reading, listening, speaking, writing), so we'll see how we can improve these for free.

VOCABULARY

When you think about vocabulary, is the first impression that comes to mind those vocabulary tests you had at school, where all you did was memorize a certain list of words for each test and forget everything as soon as you were done?

What a stressful, ineffective way of learning vocabulary! This was one of the key reasons I wanted to avoid learning a new language, and I'm sure you can relate to that. So how can we learn vocabulary differently?

The first visual that comes to mind is a dictionary. We live in an era where free dictionaries can be found online. What's more, it's easier than ever to search for a word and its definition, or how it's used in your target language; plus, we can find examples of this word in context. That's so convenient, isn't it?

But what if you're not into dictionaries? Are you shaking your head in disapproval as you read these lines? Fortunately, a dictionary isn't the only way to improve your vocabulary. It's a tool to turn to when in we're in need, not something we should open up and study, like a textbook.

If we all know someone who speaks our target language—be it a friend or a family member—then we have access to new vocabulary more frequently. If we live in a country where people speak our target language, then new vocabulary is everywhere. We often don't even have to look for it.

But how is it possible to find new vocabulary to learn online for free? And how do you make all that new vocabulary stick?

Let's dive right in now.

REPETITION, REPETITION, REPETITION

"Review your vocabulary," your language teacher used to say. "There's a test coming up."

"Time to go over the formulas again," advised the science teacher before handing you a new set of exercises to do. Teachers generally insist on reviewing what you've learned. And they're absolutely right!

Our brains love repetition because it helps new concepts stick and solidifies new memories. That's why professional basketball players make hundreds or thousands of shots per day to improve their shooting percentage. It's why musicians practice scales over and over again. To make sure the new information stays fresh in your mind, you need to review it from time to time; otherwise, it'll l most likely vanish.

This is where the Spaced Repetition System (SRS) comes in. It's a method that gives you the new information before you can forget it so that it's always there when you need it. That way you can memorize new words and phrases and never forget them! How does that work?

When you find the right time interval between each recall, you can remember more by spending less time studying. Rather than cramming it all once and repeating it as often as possible, you distribute your efforts over time in a way that the information always stays active in your head. You can either find the right intervals yourself through practice, or you can have SRS software calculate them for you.

Let's see how we can use SRS to learn vocabulary for free.

FLASHCARDS

Flashcards are pieces of paper with a word or a phrase in your target language written on one side and its translation in your native language on the other. To study them, you review both sides. Let's look at one example of how you can use flashcards to learn vocabulary.

First, create flashcards with the new words you want to learn. Use small pieces of paper so that you can easily flip them. Write each word or phrase in your target language on one side and the translation in your native language on the other.

Use separate boxes or designated spaces so that you can put the flash cards there before and after you review them. Each box represents a different time interval. For example, in one box you'll put the flash cards you want to review every day, another box for every other day, one for every week, and so on. The more easily you can remember a flashcard, the less often you'll have to review it.

Start by putting all the flashcards in a one box. This will be the box where you'll store all the new flash cards you haven't reviewed yet.

Take the first flashcard, look at the side of your native language, and try to think of its translation in your target language. It's more effective to test yourself on your target language rather than your own, especially if you want to learn how to speak or write in your target language. If you just want to understand a language, then do it the other way around.

If you successfully remember the translation, move it to the next box (the one with the shortest time interval); if you don't remember it, the card remains in the first box. Then review the box with the shortest time interval, and if you get a card right, move it to the next box. If you fail to recall it, send it back to the first box, no matter which box it was in before.

Repeat the process until all the flashcards end up in the same box, the one containing everything you can successfully remember.

You can use flashcards not only for vocabulary, but also for anything else you wish to memorize, like grammar rules if you like learning about them.

Flashcards are easy to create and you can take them everywhere. Just organize them into decks and take some with you while you're waiting somewhere or when you're on the bus, etc.

Fortunately, that's just the analog way of going about SRS. If you choose to go the digital way, there's a lot of software out there to help you. Most apps and sites for vocabulary are based on SRS, and they calculate your spacing schedule for you so that you don't spend too much time figuring out how often you should review the new vocabulary. Let's look at some examples of SRS-based software.

ANKI

Anki is one of the most popular SRS software out there, including among language learners. With Anki, you import ready-made decks of cards with new words to learn or create your own, and the system quizzes you on them. If you remember a card well, you can ask Anki to test you much later on it. If you got it right but it wasn't so easy, you can ask to review it a bit more often. The harder it is for you to remember a card, the more often Anki will show it to you. If you get a card right over and over again, the time interval will increase and you won't see it again any time soon. If you can't remember a card well, Anki may ask you again, even during the same study session. Anki is free everywhere, except on the iPhone, but there are other free alternatives if you have an iPhone (check out Brainscape or Tinycards, which have similar features to Anki).

MEMRISE

Memrise is a platform (and an app) that has language learning courses designed to help you learn vocabulary. There are courses in many languages, and you can choose what appeals to you the most. For each new word or phrase, you can create your own memes so that you can remember them easier, and you can also create your own courses where you can import any words and phrases you want to learn. Memrise uses SRS to determine how often you should review the new pieces of vocabulary. There's a free and a paid version, but the free version is more than enough to get you going. The downside is that you don't have full control over what words you learn, but you can solve this by creating your own course in the platform.

DUOLINGO

Duolingo is a site that teaches languages for free and gamifies the whole process. All you have to do is choose the language you want to learn and start translating words and phrases the course gives you to improve your use of the language. The more you advance, the harder the sentences get. You continue until you finish the whole course and get a grasp on the language you want to learn. Duolingo can help you learn new vocabulary in a fun way. It can also teach you to study every day by awarding you points, and by letting you know if you're on a streak and how many days you've been learning.

I tried this platform for Spanish for a few months after it came out, and it taught me to learn something new in my target language every day and to have fun, but it wasn't enough for me. Because of that I looked for other methods to use at the same time. Just like on Memrise, the downside is that you don't have full control of what you learn, and Duolingo gives you phrases that you may find useless and uninteresting; however, if you don't learn them, you can't advance in the course.

CLOZEMASTER

Clozemaster is an online resource that helps you build your vocabulary and learn new words and sentences in context. It's designed like a video game, and has exercises where you have to choose or fill in the missing word. It's available as an app for smartphones and tablets, and as an online website. While this resource is suitable only for upper beginner or intermediate level learners, it's quite addictive and fun to use. You can easily learn lots of new words in context and even collect useful phrases, but, as with Memrise and Duolingo, you don't have full control here either. There's a free version you can use indefinitely, and it's available in a wide range of languages --- even Guarani or Latin.

So now that you have a few examples to consider, how do you make the most out of SRS software and gain full control of what you learn?

BECOMING THE MASTER OF YOUR SRS

As we saw, Anki and Memrise let you create your own flashcards and courses. Since this takes more time, you might be tempted to use the tons of ready-made flash cards and courses you can find on these platforms. The problem is that a lot of them come without context; they're just isolated words and phrases. Although you'll be able to remember them successfully, it's highly unlikely you'll use them while speaking the language.

To get the most out of SRS programs, you have to think of them as a place where you can insert your own words and phrases to learn—a white wall waiting for you to paint it the way you want so that you can use it.

By doing it this way, you can choose phrases that you know you'll eventually use when speaking, or new words in context. You can find that material by using the methods we previously discussed about collecting language material.

Do you want to speak about your favorite hobby? Create a deck of flashcards or a course with all the possible phrases you could use to talk about it, and let the software help you remember everything. Want to learn new words from an interesting article you read and put them to use? Copy the sentences where you found the words and put them in a new course with the article's title as a name.

You can get a lot better in a language just by jotting down all the interesting phrases you come across, inserting them into an SRS software so that you don't forget them, and putting them to use, either by speaking to people or writing.

Many people swear by SRS for these reasons and deem it absolutely necessary for successful language learning. But, as I repeatedly stress throughout the book, no method is perfect; no method is absolutely necessary. What works for me might not work for you, and that's exactly how it should be.

For example, so far in my language learning journeys, I've made use of SRS but haven't relied on it too much because it bores me easily. So while I might spend a week or two doing Anki every day, that's usually all it takes for me to ditch it and use other methods for vocabulary instead. Don't be afraid to ditch a method and use another if it doesn't work for you.

But what other methods are there to improve vocabulary? Let's have a look at some.

STICKY NOTES

Back in Greece, I used to paper the walls of my room with sticky notes bearing words in my new language for everything I saw—as well as useful sentences I wanted to learn. Sticking them on my walls meant that I could see them every day and make them stick.

Can't remember the word for "fridge" in your new language? Post a sticky note to that appliance where you'll see it all the time, and you'll solve your problem! You can also stick sentences on your wall, and whenever you feel like they've stuck in your head for good, replace them with different ones. If you don't switch them out, you run the risk they'll become a part of your home's decorations, and you'll hardly notice them after some time. Like SRS, this method also relies on repetition, which helps the new words and concepts stick in your mind.

Repetition can do wonders for our vocabulary skills in numerous other ways, too.

CONTEXT CLUES

Sometimes words stick passively. For example, while reading, we come across a word that already seems familiar to us, and we think, "Hey, I've seen this word somewhere else. I know what it means." Chances are, this happens even though you've never actively tried to learn that word and make it stick. You simply looked for its translation once and have come across it so many times ever since that it's become second nature. You see that word often, even though you want to learn something else or you're just reading a text to find out what it's about, and one day, bam! It sticks!

This is an excellent way of learning new words (or even grammar, as we'll see later). Also, the more often you're exposed to the same word, the more necessary it is that you know it. If it appears in texts, sounds, or videos time and time again, it must be a common word.

When you travel to the country where your target language is spoken, you learn through immersion like this—you hear a word or a phrase over and over again, and you finally learn it passively. You can also benefit from this method without having to travel anywhere, as I often did when I was still in Greece learning languages like Basque or Catalan, which no one around me ever spoke.

So how can you learn new words that way, through this immersion-type method?

One great way is by listening to music. If you love certain songs and you listen to them repeatedly, you'll most likely experience this and add quite a few new words to your passive vocabulary. If you keep following that process, you might find yourself actually using these words to talk to people.

This has happened to me numerous times. I'd shamelessly use phrases I'd heard in songs during a conversation. Sometimes I was even caught, which made the whole conversation even more fun, as we discovered we had a common taste in music.

Another way is by reading in your target language, and we'll cover this in more depth in the "Reading" chapter.

So if you prefer learning through immersion rather than SRS, perfect! The only downside I can see is that it might take more time to actually learn new words, but hey—they'll most definitely stick without too much extra effort as you acquire them naturally.

THE MOST COMMON WORDS

Another way to learn new words and find out what words you should learn is by starting with the most common words in your new language. If you google "most common words in X language," chances are you'll find a list with 100, 500, 1,000, or even 2,000 or more common words in your new language. From there, you can choose words to learn and write sentences or stories with them. If you don't know what kind of sentences to make, you can use Reverso Context or Tatoeba to see how a word is used in context and pick the sentences you'll most likely use. Some people find that learning the most common words first is a great way to boost your speaking skills early on, as you'll learn only certain words you'll most likely use and you can be creative by combining those words into sentences. So, if you want to start small and let your creativity run riot, starting with the most common words might work for you.

If you're tech savvy or if you simply like organization, you can make a spreadsheet (e.g., in Excel) and list the words, the translations, and an example sentence for each word. Then you can separate the words into groups and try to make sentences containing all the words of each group. The possibilities are endless! Who knows … maybe you can say a lot of things by using just five or six common words in all possible combinations!

STORYTELLING

If you have a certain set of words and phrases you want to learn, you can come up with a story that includes all of them. Simply try to put all the words and phrases you want to learn into sentences, and then tell the story out loud to yourself, to a learning partner, or write them down.

If these words aren't really related to each other and it's hard to make a story that makes sense, fear not. The crazier the story sounds, the easier it'll be for you to remember! Let your imagination run wild and think of a story that includes all of them. If you come up with, say, a giant crocodile that had a pizza on its head and wanted to cook fake mermaids—no problem at all. You might have a very strange image in your head, yet you'll be able to remember all those words.

Alternatively (and especially if you're not the creative type), you can use a story that already exists and try to inject the new words and phrases in it.

MNEMONICS

Here's where your native language (or a language that you already know) comes into play! If a new word reminds you of something in your own language, you can use this to your advantage and let it help you remember the new word.

When a word sounds like something in your native language, do your best to associate them with one another in your mind. Memrise can help you with that, as you are free to associate your own memes to each new word or phrase so that you can retain it.

For example, the word for "want" in Hungarian is "*akar*," so I'd always think of the phrase, "I want AKAR (which reminds me of "a car")" and I'd picture a huge car with a Hungarian flag on it and me sitting behind the wheel, traveling across Hungary. The more vivid and full of emotions and imagination your mnemonics are, the easier it'll be for you to remember the new words!

Simply take a list of words and phrases you want to learn and try to come up with mnemonics for them. Keep that list short so that you don't get overwhelmed, and see whether your mnemonics help you memorize new words effectively. Please note that you don't need a mnemonic for every word you encounter; you can just use it for the words that are harder for you to remember.

Alternatively, instead of associating with words in your native language, you can associate images to new words, especially if you're a visual learner. But whatever you choose to do, make sure to …

BE CREATIVE AND HAVE FUN!

Creativity and fun always help to learn and sustain new concepts.

One of my favorite methods to improve vocabulary is to try to translate a well-known song from my native language into my target language and see if the new lyrics fit the song. It gets even more fun when you translate everything literally, word for word.

I had a similar session in Spanish with some friends of mine who are also Spanish learners, and we had a long night of laughing and singing well-known Greek songs literally translated to Spanish. Apart from the immense fun we had, we learned a lot of new words and phrases! So don't be afraid of being a little more creative if it means having fun with the language and learning new words at the same time.

If you're into music and singing in general, you can also choose to sing the new vocabulary you want to learn while you do something that doesn't need much thought, like household chores or driving to and from work. Just make sure you're alone or with another learner; otherwise, it might get a bit too uncomfortable for people around you.

If, on the other hand, you like art, you can use it to learn vocabulary as well! Simply draw a picture of a word or phrase, write the word or phrase next to it, and stick it somewhere that you can see it every day. The funnier and crazier the picture, the easier it'll be for you to remember the word it depicts.

BRAINSTORMING

Think about one topic you'd like to know how to talk about. It could be your favorite hobby, the weather, your profession, or current affairs, for example. After you choose one topic, try to brainstorm the words you believe you'd need to talk about it with someone, look them up in your target language, then write them down in your notebook (or on your phone or your PC) under the topic you want to talk about. You can then see whether this helps you find new words and remember them more easily. You can also write a short paragraph on that topic using these new words.

MAKE YOUR OWN SENTENCES

How about putting the new words into action right from the start? We've already explained how your brain learns and remembers phrases more effectively than words, as well as how learning phrases helps you know how to use them in context. Simply try to make a sentence with each new word you encounter. It doesn't have to be long; you can use just two to five words if you want, and you can make more than one sentence for a word until you feel you know the full meaning of that word. You can then look up the new sentences to see if a native speaker would use them, too.

I'VE HEARD THAT BEFORE! - COGNATES

Cognates are words in different languages that mean the same thing and look almost the same. Think of the word "banana," which is the same in a lot of languages, or "impossible" in English, which becomes "*imposible*" in Spanish and "*impossibile*" in Italian, etc. This happens either because the words share a common root word or because words are loaned between languages.

You can use cognates to your advantage to learn new words more easily. If you're a Spanish speaker wanting to learn Italian, you can benefit from this a lot and accelerate your learning. Because these two languages share a common root (they both come from Latin), you'll come across similar words more often than not. You can even think of a Spanish word and try to make it sound more "Italian," and chances are you'll be correct.

Even if you're learning a language from an entirely different language family than your own, you can still find cognates and use them to expand your vocabulary.

One caution for this method, though, is "false friends," which are words that seem very similar but mean something else. A famous example is "*Estoy embarazada*" in Spanish. It's very tempting to think that this means "I'm embarrassed" in English because, let's face it, they sound very similar. What it actually means, however, is "I'm pregnant." False friends don't happen too often, though, as almost 90 percent of the cognates share the same meaning.

GOOGLE TRANSLATE

Google Translate has a bad reputation because its translations of entire articles or even paragraphs can be problematic, given that it doesn't pick up on context. For isolated words, phrases, and short sentences, however, it can be very reliable.

Play with an English sentence in Google Translate. Try changing the verb, the grammatical tense, the subject, and the object and see how each change affects the translation in your target language. Also, try to add words you haven't learned yet to the sentence. This can help you learn a lot. If you don't understand what Google Translate proposes, you can google the part you don't understand to find out more about it. As soon as you finish experimenting, try googling the final sentence or use HiNative to see whether native speakers actually use it.

Experimenting with the new words in a sentence can help you remember them and see them in context.

USE MEDIA

Movies, TV shows, books, podcasts, and songs aren't only great sources for the most common words, but they can also help you memorize the new vocabulary because each new word is always associated with a scene, person, or (real-life) event. Because of this, I encourage you to try to read books or watch movies in the original language (with subtitles) and figure out what the words mean. If you see or hear a phrase or sentence you don't understand, write it down, look it up, and start memorizing it using any memorizing method we've talked about so far.

USE YOUR SENSES

Using your senses can go a long way toward making the new words and phrases stick in your mind. Let's look at one example of how this would work.

You can use your mouth (taste) to say the new phrase out loud. You can use your ears (hearing) to listen to the phrase (if you've collected it from a video; otherwise, you can ask native speakers to pronounce it online on Rhinospike, a website that allows you to write a phrase in your target language and have native speakers pronounce it for you.). You can use your hands (touch) to write the phrase somewhere, and finally, you can use your eyes (vision) to read the phrase.

I left out the sense of smell, but you can also use that if the new phrase you want to learn represents something that smells pleasantly (you wouldn't want to do that with things that don't smell nice, I'm sure). There are even people attaching certain smells to memories (myself included), so maybe you could use this to learn a new phrase, especially if that phrase has any connection to a past event of significant importance to you? Using as many senses as possible helps a lot when it comes to learning new words, phrases, and concepts.

The more effort you put into processing new information, the better your chance of remembering it. Each new association is a new "mental hook" that you can attach to a piece of information. Such associations create a rich web of connections, which make later retrieval much easier.

USE SOCIAL MEDIA

Get on Facebook and start following a page you like but in your target language. Read the comments under the posts. Is there any cool word or phrase you'd love to have in your arsenal? Note down everything that interests you and look it up. Then use it in one of your essays or talk about it. You can do the same using other websites. You can also use social media (like Twitter or Instagram, for example) to search for hashtags of words you've just learned to see how native speakers use them. You might also find interesting images attached to that word. If you like using images to learn words, this is perfect. Finally, you can change the language of every social media platform you use to your target language. That way you'll expose yourself to it every day, and learn useful words like "share", "mention" etc.

GENERAL VOCABULARY TIPS

No matter which method or methods you choose to use to improve your vocabulary skills, here are some tips to keep in mind when learning vocabulary.

CONTEXT IS KING

Always learn from context because one word can have different meanings. The context that surrounds the word makes the meaning clear, not the word by itself.

Think of the word "tear" in English, for example. If you were to learn this word without context, you might learn only one meaning of it and wouldn't be able to use it in context. You'd learn that it refers to what falls from our eyes when we cry, and that's it. Then, you'd see it in a phrase such as Ronald Reagan's all-time famous, "Mr. Gorbachev, tear down this wall!" and you'd become completely confused. What do tears have to do with a wall? Could it be the Wall of Tears? That sentence doesn't even make any sense!

That's why context is king and why you need to learn sentences, not words. If you can find or create sentences that somehow show the meaning of the new word, even better. Try to find sentences where the only unknown word is the one you want to learn, so that it's easier for you to remember both the sentence and that word. So, for example, if you don't know the word for "bought", you can use the sentence "I bought a new shirt" in your target language, as long as you already know the words for "new" and "shirt". This is also a phrase you would likely use in a conversation.

It's a lot more effective to use a new word in context and learn the entire sentence, so that you have an example of how the word works in context from the get-go. As we saw, a beneficial way would be to learn a new word in a sentence of no more than five words that you know already. To find such sentences, follow the guidelines for "Collecting Language Material," or go to Reverso Context, bab.la or Tatoeba to find phrases containing the word that interests you.

Now that we understand that one of the most effective ways of learning new phrases is to use them in context, how about … reading?

The most effective way to regularly encounter new vocabulary is to read as often as possible. That way you get to see new words in context. Whatever your current language level, I suggest that you develop a habit of reading regularly in your target language. To make the most out of reading, please refer to the "Reading" chapter under this section.

I also encourage you to avoid word overload. Don't go crazy and try to memorize sixty words a day. Our brains can't take too much information all at once, and if you do manage to do it while you're practicing or studying, you'll probably forget it as quickly as you learned it.

Try to use a new word in a sentence. Then don't forget to go out and use that word again and again in real life.

Keep a notebook (physically or digitally) where you can write down words and phrases of interest at all times, especially when searching for a word that you don't know so that you can find its translation at a later time. This will save you a lot of time wondering what to learn next, and you'll have all the words and phrases that interest you handy at all times.

Studies have shown that it's more effective to memorize new words when you use context to learn them. It's easier to learn the word "read" if it's in a small sentence like "I read a book" than it is to learn just "read" or "to read." As we saw, the best method is to learn small sentences and phrases with only one or two unknown words. You don't want to clutter your phrase too much because that makes it harder to memorize.

Are you thinking, "Memorize? How do I learn to memorize something?"

We have two types of memories: our short-term memory and our long-term memory. When we encounter a new word or phrase and we study it, it enters our short-term memory. To transfer it into our long-term memory, we have to use other methods and wait a bit longer. Once a new concept enters your long-term memory, though, it's highly unlikely you'll forget it.

Okay, now we know that there are two types of memories and that we'll use phrases instead of words, but how can we make them stick? How can we transfer them from our short-term to our long-term memory?

There are actually many ways to do that, and one of them is by using spaced repetition.

With every word or phrase that you learn, imagine a situation in which you could use it. If you were taught languages like I was, chances are you never even considered how to put a new word to use; you just memorized it because you had to do so. This is why I hated vocabulary so much. We only seemed to need to learn them to ace the tests!

However, as soon as I started thinking of how to put new words and phrases to use and began looking up ways native speakers used these phrases on the Internet, I grew to love vocabulary. I realized why it's so important.

I greatly enjoy visualizing myself using certain "high-level" words in real life. I do this while talking to myself (more on that later), and this is how I usually make new words stick.

Now that you have all these ways you can teach yourself vocabulary for free, let's move on to see how you can turn this new bunch of words and phrases you've learned into longer sentences that make sense.

GRAMMAR

Grammar is one of my favorite parts of a foreign language. At the same time, I absolutely despise grammar rules. You might be asking, how is that combination possible?

We've been taught at school that studying grammar means two things: learning grammar rules and memorizing tables. I don't know about you, but I find these two tasks utterly boring, not to mention useless.

Ask any native speaker of your target language (who isn't a linguist or academic of some sort) about grammar rules in one's own language. I believe this person will be unable to explain any of the rules they were forced to memorize at school—not one of them. And yet, here they are, speaking their native language fluently like it's their own. Oh… wait, it is their own.

Turns out that rules aren't that necessary after all. Is teaching the grammar rules of your native language easy for you? No? But it's your language, and you use it every day, which means you know grammar in practice. So why should you have to learn grammar rules in your target language?

Granted, if you love learning grammar rules, then by all means, do so. But if you don't, fear not; there are other ways you can learn grammar.

Grammar is a lot more than just rules and tables. As we saw, grammar is the skeleton of the language that holds everything together. It carries the vital organs (vocabulary), so that they function like they should.

FEEL THE GRAMMAR

You can get a feel for the grammar of a language as soon as you notice a common pattern among different sentences. For example, in Spanish:

Yo tengo una gata. I have a female cat.

Hablo con ella. I talk to her.

Take a look at these two sentences and their translations, and you'll notice some common patterns. For example, both verbs end in *o* and they talk about me (the speaker)—what I do. However, only one of them has the word *yo* (*I*) inside. From this tiny detail, I can deduce that in Spanish you can omit the word *I* in a sentence, unlike English. Finally, I notice that *her* and *female cat* are both feminine, and in both sentences, the corresponding words end in *a*. So maybe a word ending in a is a female entity?

That's how you can get a feel for the grammar of a language.

Of course, what you can do at this point is use Google to research whether your hypotheses are actually true, which leads to your discovery of the corresponding rule.

So what's the difference here? Don't you end up learning a grammar rule this way too, just as you would if you bought a grammar book and read the rule about female nouns, verbs ending in *o*, and the personal pronoun *I* that can be omitted?

Yes, you do, but there's a difference.

In the examples I gave you, *you* were the one who took extra time to notice any common patterns and see whether there's a rule for what you noticed. You asked for the rule—not the other way around. Grammar books serve you the rules, ready to be memorized, before you have any idea of how they're actually used.

Catch my drift?

When you take extra time to notice these patterns and then to question yourself or the web about whether there's a rule behind them so that you can group them together, you help your brain solidify the new memories. It also gives you a sense of accomplishment because *you* discovered these rules. No one showed them to you and told you "memorize this."

That's exactly why I love grammar—because I like to pretend I'm a real-life Dora the Explorer and I'm trying to discover the New World of my target language. The more I notice common patterns as I keep learning the language and sentences get more complicated, the easier it is to actually *feel* and *assimilate* the new grammar without having to memorize a thing.

I do this repeatedly, and finally, the new grammar becomes second nature.

Try to think of something that you discovered as a kid. For example, maybe you noticed that whenever there were darker clouds in the sky, that meant it'd most likely rain? How did it feel when you realized it and you were proven right? This phenomenon is obvious to grown-ups, but as soon as you solve it by yourself and then ask a grown-up if it's true and they confirm it, you feel *absolutely fantastic!* Plus, it's highly likely that you won't forget about it since you connected an emotion to it.

This method is surely more interesting than just finding that information in a book while you were looking for something else, reading it, and then moving along.

Connecting emotions to new concepts makes them easier for you to remember. And by "discovering" grammar (rather than just opening a book and reading about it), you help yourself get used to it faster, *and* you have fun in the process because, like a kid again, you discover new rules you didn't know existed!

So go, kiddo! Time to discover the New World of your Target Language!

Try to find two or three random sentences in your target language, and see if you can find a common pattern there and what you can infer from it.

Granted, there might be exceptions that may prove you wrong. You may notice a common pattern that isn't actually a true pattern; it was just pure coincidence.

For example, you might deduce from the Spanish sentences above that all female nouns end in *a*. If you research it, you'll find out that most nouns ending in *a* are indeed female, but there are exceptions: words like *el programa*, *el panorama*, and *el clima* prove you wrong. These are all male nouns ending in *a*.

Now you've just realized you can't rely on this common pattern to tell whether a noun is female. But hold on! In most cases you were right—and you discovered the exceptions by yourself!

In this example, it was easy for me to notice one more pattern in the exceptions in Spanish. All these words come from Greek! So I deduced that if a noun ends in *a* and it's a Greek word, it's most definitely male in Spanish, not female. Bam! I used my native language to help me in Spanish!

This is why I don't agree with anyone who says we should avoid turning to our native language as much as possible—if not completely—to learn a foreign language. After all, kids have no other language to turn to when they're learning their native language, but we're adults. As adults we can use our native language as an advantage that kids don't have.

If we notice common patterns between our target language and our native language, we can connect them so that they become second nature more easily.

Another example for me is German and Greek. German has many similarities to Greek, especially regarding grammar and syntax. Let's look at an example:

Ich frage dich. I ask you.

Ich gebe dir etwas. I give you something.

We notice German has two different words for *you* in these two sentences. Why? Let's bring out our inner Dora the Explorer to help us. Do you notice any difference between the two sentences, other than the words for *you*? Yes, there's an extra *etwas* in the second sentence. The first is just "I ask you," but the second is "I give you *something.*" So maybe German makes a distinction between these two *yous* because of this word.

Well, as I speak Greek, it's much easier for me to get a feel for that grammar and make it second nature for me because, in Greek, we also make that distinction between the two *yous* for the same verbs.

So the two sentences above would be translated almost exactly the same in Greek, which is why I have no problem making that distinction. If I completely eliminated my native language from the equation, it would've been a lot harder for me to get a feel for the grammar there and get used to the new concepts.

In this case, we see the "Necessity" criteria as well.

Similarly, if your native language is English, you can take advantage of the many common sounds or roots of words of the two languages.

A great advantage of learning for free is that it gives you one kind of bliss no paid language course out there can ever give you: *the joy of discovering things yourself.*

That joy comes right back from your childhood to remind you how amazing it is and how much you've been missing it in your life. You can feel that joy when you travel, but you can also feel it when you learn languages.

If you need to put your perception of the grammar of your target language to the test, all you have to do is google "X online grammar exercises," where X is your target language. I'm sure you'll find what you're looking for there!

TWO-WAY TRANSLATION

This is another, more interactive variation of the method we used to notice common patterns between our native and target language. The difference is that this time you have to make an extra effort.

Let's say you have a sentence in your target language (Spanish, for example) and its translation in English. The first step is to try to translate the original sentence to English without looking at the English translation.

Once you've written the translated sentence, you'll have a sentence in Spanish and another sentence, which is your translation to English. Cover the Spanish sentence, and try to translate your sentence back to Spanish without looking. Then compare your translated Spanish sentence with the original Spanish sentence.

Do you see any differences? If you do, those differences indicate exactly what you haven't fully learned in your target language and what you have to work on. For example, consider the following sentence in Spanish:

Nos encontramos en la calle.

If you're learning Spanish, try to translate it to English. Once you're done, try to find the correct English translation and compare the two. (The online dictionary called Spanishdict can help you with that).

The English translation is this: We met on the street.

Now cover the Spanish version and try to translate this back to Spanish.

If you're a beginner in the language, it's highly likely that you'll come up with the following sentence:

Encontramos en la calle.

You'll have omitted the word *nos* because having that extra word makes no sense in English—but it makes perfect sense in Spanish. Why? Maybe there's hidden grammar there somewhere? There is; these verbs are called reflexive verbs.

Also, you may come across the English translation "We meet on the street" for the same sentence. This is also correct because *nos encontramos* is written the same way for present and past tenses. This discovery may lead you to a verb conjugator to see if this is the case (more on that later).

I hope that you find—as I have—that this two-translation method is a very effective way of becoming familiar with the new grammar and of testing yourself. Now let's move on to something that requires less effort.

HAVE NATIVE SPEAKERS COMPLETE THE SENTENCES FOR YOU

This is a method I really enjoy. Whenever I come across a word or phrase that I don't know exactly how to use in context, I simply google it, so that I can have native speakers do that for me without even asking.

How does this work?

Let's say I already know the phrase *estoy a punto*, which means "I am about to." I want to say, "I'm about to finish something," but I don't know how to say that in Spanish. I know that *finish* is *terminar* and *something* is *algo*, but how do I connect that with *estoy a punto*? *Estar a punto terminar algo* doesn't sound like it makes much sense. I remember I have to add a little word there because that's how I learned *estoy a punto*, but I forgot what that word was.

One way to find out is simply to google the following phrase:

"Estoy a punto"

Notice the quotation marks? That's not random. I want to search for the phrase inside quotation marks so that I can find an actual sentence that contains this phrase. Then I'll be able to see the little word I'm looking for, according to what native speakers out there say.

When I google this phrase, I find the following results:

"Estoy a punto de dejar a mi novio"

"Estoy a punto de morir de risa"

"Estoy a punto de viajar"

Now, I haven't found anything with *terminar*, which is the verb I wanted to use, but hey! I found that little word I forgot! It's *de*! So what happens now if I google "Estoy a punto de terminar"? Do people use that?

I find a lot of results with this phrase, so yes, people use that. Bingo! I learned exactly what I wanted to learn without having to ask anyone or buy any textbook; I just did two or three Google searches. Also, I discovered it myself. I answered my own question. Awesome!

This sentence goes right into my notebook because I know I'll use it. After all, as I'm writing this book, I know I haven't finished it, but if a Spanish friend of mine asks me how the book is going, I can tell him or her, "*Estoy a punto de terminar mi libro.*" How cool is that?!

So keep in mind that whenever you need context to understand how any word or phrase is used, Google is your friend.

WORDREFERENCE FORUMS

The Wordreference forums have saved my life many times when I've had doubts about grammar. The users there ask specific questions about grammar and about how certain words are used, so if you're unsure when to use a specific word and when to use another, you'll most likely find that question there. You can always ask your own questions there too, and native speakers will answer. No matter what language you're learning, I'm sure you'll find answers to some of your questions there.

WHAT ABOUT VERB TABLES?

If you're interested in how to conjugate a verb in all tenses, fear not. There are online verb conjugators that allow you to insert any verb and the site will conjugate it for you. Simply google "X online conjugator" where X is your target language.

To make the most of the conjugators, don't try to learn everything that will appear in those verb tables. You can use the "Necessity" criteria here too. Work on learning the *I* and *you* forms of the verbs that interest you so that you can use them immediately in a conversation with another person. After those forms have stuck in your brain for the verbs you want, you can either learn these two forms of more verbs you may need, or you can go on to learn the *he*, *she*, *we*, and *they* forms so that you can talk about more people and things.

That's one thing textbooks taught me that I found completely boring—entire tables of all possible forms of verbs—and we had to learn everything by heart without questioning the use of learning everything at once. Why?

Learning little by little can be the best strategy you can do to improve your grammar skills early on—without memorizing a single table, without reading a single grammar rule, and without opening a single grammar book. You'll do it all by order of immediate usefulness, all at your own pace, all for free.

WHAT ABOUT IRREGULAR VERBS?

As we saw, it's always possible that you'll come across irregularities and exceptions to grammar rules, but those are special cases. For the most part, you'll have to follow certain rules, and the more you expose yourself to the language, the faster you'll get used to them.

In most languages, irregular verbs are the ones used most often, like "to be" or "to have," but because you'll inevitably use these verbs often, irregularities won't be a problem. There's a reason why the most irregular words are the most common ones. It's easier for native speakers to remember them too, through more frequent contact!

If you're like me and you're allergic to grammar tables of any kind, you can come up with more creative ways of learning irregular verbs. Just like with vocabulary, you can create songs based on them or write poems if they rhyme with each other. If you're not creative, use YouTube. Maybe you'll find songs other people have devised to learn irregular verbs?! I still remember a song I learned back in 2013 to learn the irregular past form of some verbs in Spanish. It used the melody of the well-known song "La Cucaracha." It must still be somewhere on YouTube. *"Tener es tuve, estar estuve ... "*

Who said grammar has to be boring?

LISTENING

There are a lot of reasons to fall in love with a language. One is the way it sounds. All those sounds that seem new to you, but when put together, they produce this beautiful harmony you've never heard before that somehow captivates you. The meaning of these sounds is still a mystery at first, yet a very gorgeous one.

No matter what they mean, you find that you love sitting there listening to them, as if it were another kind of music with lyrics you don't understand but that sound good nevertheless. Because you enjoy listening to it, you expose yourself more and more to those sounds.

As time passes, you begin to make sense of all these beautiful sounds that have been put together, and you can tell what these foreign people are talking about. Maybe these sounds start losing their mysterious vibe, but because you start understanding what's going on, the joy you experience is still there—it's just different. It's the joy of understanding what seemed to be such a mysterious set of noises some time ago.

Listening is one of the most important language skills. You can improve it by exposing yourself more and more to the language, expanding your vocabulary, and noticing how people actually speak as opposed to how your traditional textbooks say they speak. This is one skill, however, that takes time to master.

In addition, there's more than one way of listening to your target language. You might want to read your favorite book in your own language and have something play in the background in your target language. You might want to go for a run and play music in your target language while you're running. You might pop a CD into your car and listen while you drive, or you can just sit down, listen to the language, and pay full attention to it, which is different from the other examples. Let's look at this in more detail.

LISTENING EXPLAINED

There are two types of listening: active and passive listening.

ACTIVE LISTENING

When you deliberately put on something in your target language and concentrate fully on it, paying attention to the words, the sounds, and what's going on, then you're doing active listening. You do no other activity; you only pay attention to the recording and try to understand what it's about. You can do active listening by watching your favorite talk show in your target language and paying attention to everything the speakers say. You can also watch a movie or your favorite video or listen to your favorite music or radio station and be fully present. As long as you're fully present, it's active listening.

PASSIVE LISTENING

When you're doing an activity—dancing, running, doing household chores, driving, or just surfing the net, for example—and you put something on to listen to in the background, that's passive listening. You still listen to your target language, but you do something else at the same time, which means you're not fully present.

With that said, you shouldn't completely avoid passive listening because it's always helpful to expose yourself to the sounds of your target language and gradually get used to them. It's just that listening to the language isn't the most effective use of your time. If you really want to improve your listening comprehension effectively, you should opt for active listening.

Let's see how you can use the two types of listening in practice.

HOW TO IMPROVE YOUR LISTENING SKILLS

There are plenty of ways to improve your listening skills.

One very effective way would be to find a source you can listen to as well as the transcripts of that source so that you can read along in case there's something you don't understand. By combining listening with reading, you can make sure to improve both greatly.

That source can be anything from a video about your favorite hobby or your favorite documentary, to a podcast that interests you, your favorite music, or a conference talk in your target language. We'll talk about sources and where to find them later.

As long as you can find subtitles in your target language, the lyrics of your favorite music, or a transcript of the conference talk you're interested in, you also have your text ready. Just make sure that this source is not long in duration because you're going to have to listen to it more than once.

Let's see what steps you have to take.

STEP 1: LISTEN TO THE SOURCE

As soon as you choose your source, listen to it a couple times without looking at the text at all, just to see what you can understand from the language and so that you can start getting used to it. You may or may not hear words and phrases you understand already. The ones you don't understand don't matter for now; just ignore them and keep listening until the sound becomes more familiar to your ears. By "familiar"

I don't mean that you have to listen until you understand everything; right now you shouldn't care about finding out what unknown phrases and words mean.

STEP 2: COMBINE SOURCE WITH TEXT

After you've done this very critical part, then start listening to it while looking at the text in the same language. Don't translate anything from the text you don't understand yet; just keep listening while reading it. You may recognize more words this time because you heard them when you were listening without looking at the text.

STEP 3: TRANSLATE WHAT YOU DON'T UNDERSTAND AND REPEAT

Once you're done with the previous step, note the words and phrases you don't understand, and translate them so that you can fully understand what your source is about. Then listen to the source while you're reading the original text, without the translations.

STEP 4: LISTEN TO THE SOURCE AGAIN

Finally, listen to your source without looking at the text. Doesn't everything sound a lot more familiar to you now?

As long as you find a very interesting source so that you don't get bored listening to it over and over again, this technique can do wonders for your listening skills, and it's a technique you can use everywhere and for free.

If you follow this procedure and use it a little bit every day, you'll gradually and more easily understand how the language is used in real circumstances. When I say "real circumstances," I'm referring to the contexts in which the language is spoken by people for people who either speak it as their native language or who speak it fluently as non-native speakers.

So where can you find such resources? Let's find out.

CHOOSING LISTENING MATERIAL

To choose listening material, you have to consider yourself and why you're learning the language. In what situations do you imagine yourself using the language? What interests you the most? Once you've answered those questions, choose your materials accordingly. That way you'll drastically improve your understanding of these topics and learn useful vocabulary, which sets you up for successful conversations about these topics.

If you focus on comprehension, choose material intended for native speakers so that it's spoken at a normal, native speed. If you don't understand anything that's being said, look for transcripts or subtitles to read as you listen and follow the process outlined above.

You can use material intended for language learners if you're an absolute beginner. If you want to concentrate on improving your vocabulary and conversation skills, choose something slightly above your level.

Also, it's a good idea to prioritize. Decide if you still want to enjoy the content. Listening might get a bit boring if you stop every two seconds to write down some vocabulary. I try to find the balance by setting myself a target of how many chunks of words I want to find.

YOUTUBE

YouTube is the most famous online video-sharing platform where users can find or upload videos about anything. You can find short videos there about lots of topics in your target language, and many also have subtitles. How-to videos and parts of movies or documentaries usually have subtitles in the same language as the one from the video. Automatically generated subtitles sadly don't cut it because they're given in the language as recognized automatically so a lot of words and phrases can be off. For this reason, you want to make sure the video has subtitles in the language and repeat the process explained above.

There are many other ways you can use YouTube to learn languages. The most obvious one is to follow channels that offer free lessons in your language of interest. No matter what language you want to learn, chances are you'll find videos with free lessons for it. There are many professors out there who are native speakers with their own channels that feature interesting, useful, and most importantly, free content.

You can also follow any channel you're interested in (provided it's in your target language), like videos with talks about your favorite hobby, documentaries, or anything that interests you.

By watching YouTube videos, not only can you hear the language and see the words they use, but you can also know exactly what they're talking about because you have subtitles in a language you know well. A very good example of videos that feature both the subtitles in your new language and in English is the Easy Languages series. These are videos with the real version of your new language as it's spoken in the streets and in everyday speech. For example, there's the Easy German series, where one or two people that speak German go out on the streets of Germany and ask passersby certain questions. Each video covers a specific topic or question, and they have subtitles in German and English that appear simultaneously in both languages.

Of course, there are YouTubers that upload videos about a wide array of topics, and these videos are for native speakers of the language. If you're an intermediate or advanced learner, you can choose to follow these channels and extract listening sources from them.

TED TALKS

You can also do the same using TED Talks. If you're not familiar with TED, it's an amazing platform of conference talks about a huge variety of topics. You can most likely find talks in your target language too, and they'll definitely have subtitles in your target language, as well as a separate transcript *and* a transcript in English (or even your native language) so that you can easily find the translations for the original text in case there's something you don't understand.

Most talks are in English, but there's a dedicated YouTube channel for Spanish called TED en Español, and the YouTube channel called TEDx Talks has a wide variety of talks in other languages. TED also enables you to use two-way translation between the original text and the translated text so that you can get used to how your target language works compared to your native language or the English text, if English isn't your native language. You can follow the steps we discussed in the "Grammar" chapter under Section 2.

As there are many talks in English, you can even watch them in English but turn on the subtitles in your target language to see how certain phrases in English are translated to your new language. Would the native speakers of your new language use the same words and structures as English, or would they be totally different? You can find phrases of interest there and jot them down in your notebook.

MUSIC

Another great collection of sources is music in your target language. With music, it's even easier to use the process explained above, as the lyrics are almost always available online, which gives you easy access to both the source and the text. It's also easier for you to make the new words and expressions stick by listening to your favorite songs. You can either use

YouTube or services like Spotify, Pandora and Amazon Music to find and listen to music in your target language.

PODCASTS

Podcasts are also very useful resources for language learning. If you have a smartphone or an mp3 player, you can take podcasts with you everywhere. Whatever topic you can think of, there's a podcast for it. You can use Podcasts on iPhone or Pocket Casts and other apps on Android to find your favorite podcasts in your target language. You can listen to them during your "dead time," while you do household chores, or wherever, whenever. With podcasts you can immerse yourself in your target language, no matter in which country you are. And best of all, they're free! If your attention span isn't long enough, you can opt for ten-minute or even five-minute podcasts. There's a wide variety of podcasts, both for native speakers and for language learners.

If you're at a lower intermediate level in your target language, try looking for podcasts that are slightly above your level so that you can understand what's going on (for the most part) and still come up with new words and phrases you don't understand yet and want to learn. Choose some that are easy enough that you enjoy listening to them, yet difficult enough to push you to learn new things. This is how you make the most progress. If you don't understand much of what's spoken, instead of ditching it altogether (like you might do with reading materials), try finding transcripts for it and follow the process I outlined above.

ONLINE RADIO

Listening to the radio in your target language is a great way to improve your listening skills, especially if you want to improve your comprehension skills. You can use it for passive listening or to tune your ear to more and more of your target language to get used to the pace, the sounds, the intonation of the language, and to see what you can understand.

The TuneIn website and app lets you listen to thousands of stations, and you can browse stations by language and country to find stations in your target language. To make the most of online radio, choose to listen to news broadcasts or stations without music—just talk. The downside is that you won't find any transcript for what you're listening to, but it's nevertheless a good way to put your listening skills to the test and discover new vocabulary. You can spend as little as ten minutes per day listening to a radio station in your target language, and you'll see an improvement in your listening skills.

IMPROVING YOUR LISTENING SKILLS DURING A REAL CONVERSATION

Podcasts, radio, and videos are good, but what happens when you're in a real conversation with a native speaker and want to improve your listening skills? Simply follow the steps below:

Listen for keywords and deduce the meaning! If, for example, the native speaker tells you something like blahblahblah-our meeting-blahblahblah-Thursday (where "our meeting" and "Thursday" are the only words you understand), you can bet one is talking about your next meeting and whether it should be on Thursday. So if you've run out of chances to ask what they were talking about (if you're too ashamed to say "excuse me?" over and over again), you can assume the speaker wants to meet up with you on Thursday.

If the opposite happens and you understand everything a native speaker says apart from one or two words, then you can use the surrounding context to deduce their meaning.

If you hear a speaker say something interesting, then repeat it! Say, "Oh, [repeat what they said]. I didn't know you said it like that!" By repeating the phrase actively, you'll most likely remember it. If people know that you're learning their language, they won't find it weird that you repeat what they say.

Don't be afraid to ask or tell them to talk a bit more slowly. It's normal!

Try to listen to group conversations! It's often difficult and very tiring to try to understand everything, but you don't get put on the spot if you don't understand; you can focus purely on listening. I did this a lot when I first arrived in Germany; and although it was hard at first, it really helped my comprehension!

Even if you don't understand what's going on in the conversation, listen to words and phrases used repeatedly and try to note them down. Google them to see if you've noted down everything correctly, and then see what they mean and when people use them.

What if you don't understand native speakers at all though? What if having a conversation with them is extremely hard for you? Read on to find out what to do.

I DON'T UNDERSTAND NATIVE SPEAKERS!

This is the biggest problem language learners face. Even if you can barely speak your target language, there are ways you can get your message across, including throwing in a word here and there and making signs with your hands. But if you don't understand what people say to you, it's a tad harder to communicate.

Being able to understand native speakers takes time. You have to expose yourself to the language more systematically every day. Train yourself with conversations at normal speed (not slowed down for learners) from the start. Tune your ear to the new sounds and the speed they come at you. At first, everything will sound unintelligible—just a random set of sounds—but as you keep at it, your mind will gradually get used to the sounds and begin to distinguish words and phrases at normal speed.

BUT NATIVE SPEAKERS SPEAK TOO FAST!

I could have added this to the myths, but it fits well here in the "Listening" section. Every language sounds very fast when you don't understand it, but I can assure you that native speakers of any language speak at similar speeds, with only marginal differences, depending on the language.

If a language sounds too fast to your ears, this can mean two things:

- Your vocabulary is still limited, so you don't understand most of the words being spoken.

Whenever you speak the language, even if you don't know a word for something, you can try to describe it using other words that you do know, or you can let the other person guess what you're talking about. In this way, your lack of vocabulary doesn't create big problems for you when speaking. When you have to listen to the language, however, you can't choose your own words to listen to; you have to listen to the words other people choose. If you don't know these words, you get lost and can't understand what the other person is talking about, so everything ends up sounding too fast for you.

- You've learned the "book" version of the language.

This is very important, and language learners tend to overlook it. There are two kinds of pronunciation of a foreign language: standard pronunciation (the "book" version) and real pronunciation (how "real" natives speak). Standard pronunciation is what we learn in language learning books, or what we hear in documentaries like the BBC.

Real pronunciation is how the language sounds in everyday speech. I'm not talking about dialects here; I'm referring to how people actually pronounce certain words so that they can speak faster and make the language flow better.

Don't worry if you can't make the distinction; after all, that's what language learning books teach you!

Think of your native language. Do you clearly pronounce every letter of the words you use in the way they were intended to sound? Or do you shorten certain syllables and sounds so that you can speak faster? Chances are you do the latter, and you don't even realize it because all native speakers of your language do the same and you understand each other.

Think about the simple English question, "What do you want?"

In books, documentaries, and standard pronunciation, each word is pronounced fully and clearly. But in "real" pronunciation, what comes out is something that sounds like, "Waddi you wan?" Everyone understands what we're talking about, and it sounds perfectly fine. But somebody learning English needs time to get used to that pronunciation.

Think about "I am going to go there." Standard pronunciation says that each word is pronounced clearly, but real pronunciation says it's pronounced "I'm gunna go there."

This happens in other languages, too.

In the state of Germany where I live, people say "*fümundzwanzig*," instead of "*fünfundzwanzig*." They also like to eat the "ch" sound of "*auch*" in phrases like "*Ich auch nicht*," which sounds like "*Ich aunicht*."

That's exactly what native speakers of any language do! So words don't sound exactly like they were intended to sound, or like your average textbook says they sound. This creates the illusion of high-speed speech in a foreign language, even when you actually know all the words and have an advanced vocabulary. You know the "book" version of these words, but what you hear is the "real" version.

You can improve your comprehension of the "real" version of the language by exposing yourself to it so that you can see how words you already know actually change when spoken. Once you get used to the difference between the "book" version and the "real" conversational version, the speed will magically become normal in your target language. Yes, miracles do happen from time to time.

That's why it's always a good idea to avoid slow versions of your target language, as this won't help you to understand native speakers better.

Exposing yourself to the language isn't the only way to improve your listening skills though. You also have to improve vocabulary and pronunciation. Never forget the key ingredients of each language skill! If you don't know what's wrong and you can't improve one of your language skills, *always* try to see whether there's something wrong with the key ingredients of each skill, as described in the "Breaking Down Languages" chapter under Section 1.

READING

Chances are, you want to learn your target language so that you can read your favorite books in the original language. After all, no matter how good a translation is, the original language of a book simply can't be beat because that was the language inside the author's brain and that alone tells the reader exactly what the author wants the reader to know.

Maybe you want to read pages and blogs about your favorite hobby, or you're looking for original sources of a country's history and culture, or you just want to be able to read the lyrics of your favorite songs in the language and understand them?

This is where improving of your reading skills comes in.

This sounds simple, but it's a bit more complicated than it seems. You see, if you're learning Russian to be able to read Dostoyevsky in the original language, actually picking up a Dostoyevsky book in its original language and beginning to read it won't help you much. In fact, especially if you're a beginner in the language, you won't be able to turn to page 2 because almost all the words will be unknown to you.

You need to go about it smarter.

While your end goal is Dostoyevsky, you should start reading texts where you understand 80 percent of the words. That way you'll either guess the meaning of the unknown words through context, or you'll grab a dictionary and turn to page 2 much faster and easier.

Always strive for texts that interest you and are slightly above your level. That way, you'll want to keep reading, *and* you'll figure out what the unknown words mean from the context to get the full meaning of the text. If you do this, you'll be able to enjoy what you read, and you'll also learn new things at the same time.

So if it's too difficult to understand, leave it. If it's too easy, also leave it. You want to read something easy enough to understand yet challenging enough to learn new things.

But what if you're a total beginner?

Then you might want to pick up basic vocabulary first and start with very small texts—just a paragraph will do. You might also choose to postpone reading altogether until you learn some basic words and phrases, and then move on to basic texts or webpages.

At this point, you might be thinking, "Hey, my favorite books are *not* free! Am I not supposed to learn a language for free?"

Absolutely. Your favorite book will be the end goal. What can you do in the meantime?

Turn to the Internet, of course!

As we've previously discussed, your target language lives in two places: the country (or countries) where it's spoken and the Internet. If you reside in a country where people speak your target language, we'll discuss what more you can do later. If you don't dwell in such a country, however, travelling there breaches our "for free" policy, so you'll have to turn to the Internet.

All you have to do is think of what you enjoy reading online. If you surf every day, that shouldn't be hard to guess. It could be current affairs or news, or blogs about art, cars, decorations, sports, how-to, personal development—anything.

Try googling your favorite hobby in your target language to see what comes up. As soon as you find one page that seems interesting, click on it.

HOW TO TURN ANY WEBPAGE INTO LANGUAGE LEARNING MATERIAL

Okay, so now what?

You have three possibilities.

1. Read the page in your target language just as it is and try to guess what the text says. Jot down in a notebook (or copy on Notepad) all unknown words and phrases so that you can look them up later. As soon as you finish the text and you've got the gist of it, use an online dictionary for your unknown words and phrases, and choose which ones you'd like to learn. If you need to find other example sentences for a new word (making it even easier to understand that new word!), you can use Linguee, Reverso Context, or Tatoeba.

2. Install Google Translate. This is an extension that allows you to translate any language to the language you choose. It allows you to right-click or highlight any word or sentence, and the translation appears right away in the same window. That way you'll immediately see what each unknown word means as you read on. Alternatively, if your browser is Google Chrome, you can install the extension transOver.

3. Install Readlang. This is a great extension (and webpage) that allows you to click on words you don't know to see the translation, and then it saves these words to your account so that you

can review them later using flash cards. All you have to do is create an account on Readlang, choose your target and your native languages, and browse the web in your target language. Every word you click on will be automatically saved on Readlang, and you can review them later or export them to Anki. If you're not interested in reviewing certain words, you can delete them through the website and review just the ones you immediately want to learn (see "Learning by Necessity" in the "Vocabulary" chapter).

Following these guidelines enables you to turn any page out there that's in your target language into free language learning material, and the best part is that you can tailor that material to your needs! There's no need to read boring texts out of a textbook again. Just figure out what your favorite texts are, and make sure to learn them using one of these three possibilities—or all of them if you prefer.

If you keep using these techniques, the texts are going to get larger and larger, you'll learn more and more vocabulary, and one day you'll be ready to tackle that Dostoyevsky book because you'll be able to understand 80 percent of the words (or even more!).

Let's see how this works in more detail and figure out how to make the most of your reading sessions.

READING EXPLAINED

Just like listening, there are two types of reading:

1. *Reading as much as possible.* With this type of reading, all that matters is that you get the gist of what you're reading; you'll deduce the meaning of the unfamiliar words from the context around them and just read more and more. This will expose you to a lot in your new language, and it'll further challenge you as

you try to understand what the text is about. You'll have fun reading and absorb the language in a natural way, getting the feel of it the more you read. You can do this type of reading with long texts, such as articles. You're not actively looking for new vocabulary and grammar; you just want to enjoy reading.

2. *Focused reading.* With this type of reading, you're trying to fully understand the vocabulary and grammar. In this case, every word matters, so it takes a lot longer to read a text. You can take that new vocabulary and put it into your preferred method to make all new words stick, using the ways we described in the "Vocabulary" chapter. You can use this kind of reading for short texts (preferably about a specific vocabulary topic), such as transcripts of a video or a podcast, a short blog post about something that interests you, or even a tweet in the language. If you use a long text for focused reading, it'll be a long, tiring process.

The most effective way to go about it would be to combine the two types of reading with an emphasis on focused reading. Try following a Facebook page in your target language about something that interests you, and do focused reading of a post every day. If you also want to read as much as possible, go for it, but try to prioritize focused reading because this is what will help you learn more new insights about your new language.

PICKING READING TOPICS

- For reading as much as possible: pick a topic you would read about in your native language.
- For focused reading: pick something you know you would use or talk about in the future. I like to read transcripts of talks or videos about personal development. It's something I love talking about *and* would read in my native language, so I choose to do it in my target language to save time and learn more about the language simultaneously.

If you're learning your target language for a specific goal, then by all means choose to read texts related to it. If, for example, you would like to find a certain job or use your skills with colleagues that are native speakers of your target language, then choose to read texts in your field. Otherwise, you can just choose what interests you the most and you would read in your native language, and you can select to read as much as possible instead of focused reading.

FINDING READING MATERIALS

Since we're learning for free, we'll focus on free materials.

If your main goal is to learn how to speak, then opt for dialogues or text that's in the spoken version of your target language. You can find such texts in transcripts of podcasts, talks, or videos; blog posts; movie subtitles; and even comments.

If you have a solid foundation in the language and want to improve your writing skills, you can opt for articles, texts from books written in the language, academic papers, or anywhere else you can find the language in its written form.

If you're a beginner, you can opt for material designed for language learners, such as blogs that teach the language.

For reading as much as possible: Try to skim a text to see if you can get the gist of it. Don't worry if you don't understand every word; that's not the point of this kind of reading. Rather, you want to read as much as possible and understand the general context. You can perfectly enjoy and understand a text even if you don't know all the words in it; so instead of looking up words you don't understand, just keep reading!

If you don't understand most (or any) of the text, the text is way above your level, so it would be best to ditch it altogether. If you're interested in reading it, though, just save it for a later time in your language learning journey, when your level will be higher. You can even create lists of target texts you want to read at a later time and jump back to them months or even years later to see how much you've improved. This helps you enjoy small victories, such as being able to understand something you couldn't follow when you were starting, which definitely boosts your motivation.

I encourage you not to look up words and grammar at this point; but if you find something that interests you, make a note of it in your notebook and keep reading—but try to limit the times you do that. Or if you find a phrase you understand but you'd never say it that way by yourself, note it down so that you know how native speakers actually say that.

For focused reading: This is like a study session, rather than reading. You can always skim the text first to get a general idea of the content, but you'll also want to read and examine what you don't know from each sentence, be that new vocabulary, grammar, or a phrase structure you're not familiar with. Once you find what you don't know, you can note it down again or insert it in a method you prefer for remembering new words and phrases. Since you already have the new words and phrases in context, try to copy entire sentences (as long as they're not too long, like not more than six words long) to your notebook to look up and study later.

If you want to maximize the value of what you're doing, incorporate this reading strategy into your full language learning routine. For example, you can write a summary of what you've just read or have a conversation about the topic you read. You can also watch a video or listen to a podcast on the same topic to see what else you can learn about it. Having a routine that ties it all together is crucial to making faster progress in your target language.

Let's see what else you can use to improve your reading skills.

WHEN YOUR TARGET LANGUAGE MEETS YOUR OWN LANGUAGE

One way to start your reading journey in your target language is to opt for resources that are available in both your target and your native language. Simply look for websites available in more than one language, or free bilingual e-books online. You can also select a personal favorite "sport" of mine: whenever you're in a tourist attraction in the country where you live, look to see whether there are brochures about it in various languages. If there are, pick up one in your native language and one in your new language and compare the two.

You can even use the manual of the latest device you bought! Chances are your new language is also in it, so you can learn all the related vocabulary there, if this is something that interests you.

Bilingual resources (or manuals, leaflets, or anything else that interests you that you can find written in both languages) are a great way for beginners to start getting used to how the language works compared to their own language. They also help advanced learners enrich their vocabulary and grammar skills. You can also choose certain phrases and write them down in both languages so that you can later use two-way translation to improve your skills, as we discussed in the "Grammar" chapter under Section 2.

BOOKS AND BIG TEXTS

If you happen to have a book, an e-book, or some other long text in your target language that you want to read, don't try to read the whole thing (or even as many pages as possible) in one day. Chances are you'll quickly become overwhelmed and put it down. What you can do instead is read just one to two pages per day. We've talked about the importance of chunking and dividing a big goal into small achievable steps, so this is exactly what you should do in this case too. I'd recommend you stick to nonfiction because they tend to use everyday language, rather than complicated, advanced words often found in fiction books that nobody uses in everyday life.

READING IS A NATURAL SRS

If you remember the SRS programs we talked about in the "Vocabulary" chapter, then this should make sense to you the more you think of it. Reading exposes us to all kinds of words and phrases in a language, and the most common words and phrases worth learning are used more often than others. As we keep reading in our target language, we essentially review these words and phrases to the point where they become familiar and we can remember them. What's more, we always see them in context; so even if we don't know them, we can deduce their meaning from the sentences around them. So if you're not fond of SRS software, reading can be your go-to method for expanding your vocabulary.

READING FOR ADVANCED LEARNERS

All that sounds good, but what if you're at an intermediate or upper-intermediate level in your target language and you want to master it and use it just like native speakers? Let's look at the fun, interesting reading materials out there that can take you from intermediate or advanced to proficient.

Q&A SITES ONLINE

Websites featuring questions and answers can be brilliant language learning material. Not only do you gain new information on a topic that interests you, but you can also learn the language native speakers actually speak! On these forums, native speakers use slang, everyday phrases, synonyms, and trendy speak, which will give your language skills the coveted near-native status. Let's look at one example.

QUORA

Quora is by far my favorite of these and I read it every night before I go to bed to make sure all my languages stay in shape. I follow the language-specific parts for all my languages and look up answers to interesting questions online and read them. Doing this, I've learned a lot of useful phrases only natives use. If you don't know these phrases, it's hard to find them by googling, even if you google "idioms in X language." Slang changes over time and new trends emerge, so even those idioms you find online can make you sound like you live in the '80s. That's why I recommend using Q&A sites as a perfect way of staying current with idioms.

FORUMS

If you're interested in a particular hobby, it's a great idea to look for a forum about it in your target language. That's where fellow hobbyists that speak your target language live. It's a perfect way to get to know how they talk about their favorite hobby, what phrases they use, and so on. Write the word for your favorite hobby in your target language, type "forum" next to it, and use Google to see what you can find! For example, if you're learning Italian and you like football, googling "forum di calcio" gets you to forums like Forum Calcio, where people talk about football in Italian, so you can practice your reading skills and learn a lot of related vocabulary.

REDDIT

Reddit is a huge collection of forums (or "subreddits," as they're called) where people can share content and comment on others' posts. Each subreddit covers a different topic, and there are also subreddits for speakers of languages other than English. As an advanced learner, you can follow the subreddit for native speakers of your target language and read exactly how native speakers speak on a day-to-day basis. If you're at an intermediate level, you can also find subreddits of learners of your target language and see what advice and language learning content they have to offer.

LANGUAGE-SPECIFIC SITES

I'm sure you can find excellent Q&A sites and material to master any language out there. For example, if you want to master German, you can opt for Germany's biggest platform for questions and answers, Gutefrage. If you're learning Spanish from Spain and want to use it exactly like native speakers, Tenia Que Decirlo is an amazing site to help you do exactly that. This is where I learned all the slang words I use, and surprise Spanish people with. I also learned a lot about how Spaniards think. I'm sure you can find a similar site, no matter what language you want to master!

OTHER READING TIPS

If you want more exposure to the language without having to try hard to find resources, you can change the language of your phone or your computer (or any other device), as well as Facebook or any other website or app you use daily and are familiar with, to your target language. This is an easy way to read your target language every day and get used to new words and phrases naturally.

Follow news sites and pages on Facebook, Twitter, etc. so that you don't have to actively look for material; instead you can let it come to you effortlessly every day. Reading the comments under posts is also very useful if you want to collect natural-sounding sentences and get to know how native speakers use the language. If you use Q&A apps like Quora, you can also add the version in your target language so that you receive emails with questions and answers in it.

SPEAKING

There's no denying that speaking is a very important part of language learning. The more you speak, the more comfortable you get with the language. Speaking the language also helps you remember new words and phrases easier. No wonder it's one of the top priorities of successful language learners.

For some of us, though, speaking a new language can be a big obstacle. I know how dreaded a task it can be, especially during the early stages of a language learning journey.

In fact, of all language skills, this one causes learners the most stress. It's such a challenge because you not only have to put yourself out there by speaking your target language, but you also have to understand what people say to you and have the strength to move on when you make mistakes or can't keep up.

My biggest challenge has always been speaking to other people in my target language, especially to native speakers. I sometimes struggle even today, and at least part of my issue with it is that all my life I've been taught that speaking is an exam and if I make any mistakes, they'll count against me. Of course I'm afraid of it.

I still remember my exams in English. I took them in a small room, either alone or with another candidate, depending on the exam. We'd face our examiners, and there were always two. One would speak to us and the other would just sit at the back and take notes. I was always so stressed as soon as I got into that room, especially when I started speaking and saw the silent examiner's pen moving. *Was she making notes on my mistakes? Oh, gosh, what did I say again?*

Even though I passed all those exams, that fear hasn't completely left me. I've overcome it to a great extent now, but it sometimes comes back to haunt me. That's what exams did to me.

I knew nothing would happen to me if I made mistakes, but I'd always remember that silent woman taking notes and lowering my overall score in the exams; I was afraid beyond reason. No wonder I spent so many years learning English, yet struggled to speak it for a long time.

My English teacher used to say that speaking means putting all your language skills to the test, and she was right.

But it also means having fun with the language and using the language for the reasons you may have wanted to learn it in the first place: Communicating. Meeting and talking to real people. Joking and laughing with them. It's incredibly rewarding to speak in your target language, and my teacher never told me all these things.

With all those classes, tests, and exams, we forget what languages really are—a means of communication, and a tool to express ourselves, meet new people, and understand different cultures.

We want to improve our speaking skills in our target language, but at the same time, we're afraid of speaking to people.

Speaking is like driving a car though. No matter how many books you read about the parts of a car—how it works, how to start it, and how to drive it—if you don't sit behind the wheel and start it up, you can't learn how to drive. You learn to drive by doing it—learning by doing.

It's the same with speaking; we learn by doing. The only way to practice and improve your speaking skills is by speaking in the language. If that scares you so much that you think you'll never be able to do it, there are ways around it. We'll talk about them later.

First, let's examine how you can find people with whom you can practice your target language.

FINDING A LANGUAGE PARTNER

If you don't live in or can't travel to any country where people speak your target language, all is not lost. There's a plethora of ways to find people to talk to online. As long as you know where to look, it won't be that hard to find speaking partners. Let's see how and where you can do that.

ITALKI

Italki is a site where online language teachers can connect with students and schedule online language classes.

Online language classes, you say? But that's not free, right?

Right, it's not free. But you can use the site for free to find language learning partners that want to learn your native language and whose native language is your target language. All you have to do is register with the website, create your profile, and select your native language (or languages, if you have more than one) and the language you want to improve. After that, you can look for native speakers of your target language who want to learn your native language, and message them.

You can also find fellow learners of your language, if talking to native speakers stresses you out. Just make sure their level is slightly above yours, and message them. You can find this information on their profiles. If your partner speaks the language at a level similar to you or slightly higher, you can both practice your language skills and learn from your speaking partner.

So once you find someone, ask if they would be interested in helping you with your target language. If so, you can schedule online conversations with them through Skype, Facebook Messenger, or any other app or website that lets you have online conversations with others. You can select a topic to talk about beforehand, or you can just chat in the language. If they're learning your native language, you can spend half the time speaking in that language (so that you can also help them) and the other half speaking in your target language; that way, everyone's happy. Who knows, maybe you'll end up creating a nice friendship with a person from another country and even visit them sometime?! This is just one of the many awesome benefits language learning can do for you.

INTERPALS

If you not only want to speak with people, but write to them as well, you can opt for a pen pal that speaks your target language. Interpals is the place to go for that. Simply create your profile, list what language you're learning, and start sending messages to people that speak it as their native language. You can also schedule conversations if you want, just like on Italki. I know stories of people who have formed beautiful, long-lasting friendships or even relationships via that website—and, of course, people who have experienced huge improvements in their foreign language skills!

LANGUAGE EXCHANGE

If you prefer learning offline rather than online, fear not. There are ways to take that language exchange offline. Simply search for Facebook groups in your area that have to do with foreigners living in the city, exchange students, language learners in the city, or even people from the country where your language is spoken that live in the city. You can also search for language exchange groups in your area using websites like Meetup.

As soon as you come across groups like these, ask to join and post about the language you're learning and your willingness to help them with your native language. Offering to help others may help you find people in your area willing to meet up and schedule an offline conversation with you at a café of your preference.

You can also search Facebook groups of learners of a particular language, like "French learners" or anything similar. You'll most definitely find exchange partners there!

You can then take your notebook (or your device, or however you prefer to take notes) and meet that person to practice your languages. When I lived in Budapest, I did that all the time, and I met fantastic people that showed me their city and helped me to not only improve my Hungarian, but also to learn many other things about Budapest and what to see and discover there.

For both online and offline conversations, it's best to find someone who speaks your native language at a level similar to the level at which you speak your target language so that you can talk about similar things in both languages.

WHAT TO DO BEFORE AND DURING A CONVERSATION WITH A NATIVE SPEAKER

Okay, so you've found people and scheduled an online or offline conversation. What now?

You can plan the topic you'll talk about beforehand so that you can both prepare for it. If you don't know what topic to talk about, you can use Bilingua or Conversation Starters World and choose one of the suggested topics you'll find there.

Another option is to go back to your *why* behind your desire to learn your target language. Maybe a great variety of topics resonated within the reasons you formerly listed? You can also make a list of situations in which you'll use your target language. This can be your list of discussion topics, too.

If you decide on the topic in advance, you'll have time to collect words and phrases about it beforehand and learn them using any method we've described. After you've learned them, you can start thinking of how you'd put them to use in a conversation and start writing that conversation. That way, you'll not only solidify the new memories, but you'll also discover other gaps you may have, which will give you practice material to use not only in this conversation but also in future ones. In language learning—unlike what your teacher said back at school—cheating is acceptable, so you can even prepare by writing out a script to use during the conversation.

You can't possibly script entire conversations, but you can write things you know you'll say over and over again: "What did you do today?" "I'm happy I was on time today," "I went skydiving and had a great time," for example.

Remember, you're writing to replace speaking, so you have to focus on spoken language, not advanced sentences you'd only read in a book. No one speaks like that, and it'd also be hard for you to memorize.

To make the most of an online conversation, ask your language partner to note all the mistakes you make during the conversation and give it to you after the session. That way, you'll know exactly what to correct for the next time.

Now let's explore where else you can find people to talk to in your target language.

LANGUAGE CAFES

Many cities in the world have groups and sites focused on language exchange cafes, which are regular meetings for people who want to practice a certain language. The meetings usually take place at a café, bar, or restaurant in town.

Taking advantage of these cafés did wonders for my Spanish. After three months of studying Spanish on my own, I accidentally came across a Facebook group called "Language Exchange Club Athens," where people scheduled weekly meetings to practice various languages. Spanish was one of them, so I joined them!

It wasn't easy for me. I had to overcome my fears and finally say yes; but as soon as I did, I never looked back. We met at a café and started speaking Spanish right away. That was the first time I ever spoke Spanish to other people, and it went well. I started going there weekly, and that's what made my Spanish skills skyrocket. I also made new friends and became more social, gradually eliminating my fears of getting out of my house, especially during late-night hours. Language Exchange Club Athens was a lifesaver for me, and I'll forever praise it for that.

Maybe your own local language café can help you with your speaking skills, so I encourage you to give it a try. You can look for any such event in your area using Facebook or Meetup, a site created to help you do exactly that, or you can use Google and see what you can find. Do a search using the name of the city where you live and add "language exchange" or "language cafe" next to it.

GETTING CORRECTED

Some people will want to correct you, even if you're in the middle of an important sentence during a conversation, which can be both frustrating and discouraging, especially when you're not prepared for it. Don't let it put you off, though, as it's very useful. You should note down those corrections either physically or mentally because they will bring you closer to speaking more correctly, and getting corrected is better than not getting corrected at all. It's not criticism; it's merely a way to help you improve. Always assume whoever corrects you is trying to help you. If you can't take notes after a correction, just make sure you repeat the correct form of what you said—what the native speaker suggested. This will make it easier for you to remember.

Don't take it personally if a native speaker corrects you or even judges you because you made a mistake in your target language. Keep in mind that if a native speaker judges you, this says a lot about him or her. This person probably never tried to learn another language, or worse, perhaps somebody him or her them just as harshly and they eventually quit. This is very unlikely to happen, though, as most native speakers love it when foreigners try to speak their language.

TALKING TO YOURSELF

Until now, we've talked about improving your speaking skills by having conversations with native speakers or fellow learners. Without a doubt, this is one of the best ways to improve your speaking skills.

But what if you don't feel confident enough to speak to other people? What if you're too shy to look for conversation partners? What if your level is low enough that you can't keep up with a conversation, and yet you want to improve your speaking skills?

That's where self-talk comes in; it saves you from blank stares and awkward silences. Practicing self-talk means talking to yourself in your target language out loud.

Sounds weird?

Think again.

It's a very powerful tool that can not only help you greatly improve your speaking skills, but also improve other language skills and areas in your life. Don't forget that you're the most willing conversation partner that's out there!

What happens when you come across new phrases you deem useful, phrases you'd like to learn and use in the future, but there's no one around with whom you can practice them? How could you possibly learn them and try to simulate them in practice?

Talking to yourself can help you:

- Practice the language anytime you want
- Talk about anything you want
- Memorize new words and phrases more easily
- Get comfortable with the language
- Speak faster
- Sound more natural
- Find new words and phrases to learn
- Repeat phrases over and over again and improve your accent

I'll give you an example of how much this has helped me.

A few years ago, I encountered a challenge. A Basque radio show wanted to interview me online.

I'd never done any radio interviews before in any language, and now I had to do one in Basque, a language I'd started teaching myself earlier that year. And that wasn't all. I'd never had any conversation with a native speaker in Basque before! This would be my first ever. Plus, it'd be live on the radio.

Imagine having your first conversation in a new language with a native speaker while a lot of other native speakers were listening to you.

Terrifying, right?

It's petrifying, especially if you happened to be an introverted perfectionist, like I was at the time.

As if all this weren't enough, the topic of her interview would be how I'd become conversational in the language after only ten months of studying it. (I'd put up a YouTube video of myself speaking the language, and the radio show discovered it and asked to interview me.)

So, given the focus of the interview, I felt I had to prove my language skills and sound as natural as possible, even though it would be the first time I'd ever used the language to communicate with an actual person. That was a lot of pressure!

Yet the conversation went way better than I thought it would. While I did make some mistakes here and there, I had no big pauses, answered all their questions, sounded natural, and got my point across. And I owe it all to self-talk. It's what made it all possible.

How?

I felt comfortable speaking the language, and that's something people also noticed in my YouTube video—and later, in person.

It helped me handle the most stressful first conversation with a native speaker far better than I could've ever imagined.

I improved my speaking skills without having to look for native speakers or fellow learners with whom to practice. That was too hard for Basque anyway.

I found an efficient way to become better at speaking, free of charge. It's also guilt-free, as you'll be the only one to hear any mistakes you make.

Talking to yourself lets you practice speaking anytime you want, and you can talk about any topic out loud (although doing this in public might feel too weird, so just find a place where nobody else can hear you and simply start talking to yourself).

At first, it's normal to feel overwhelmed about what to say. You might wonder, "How does this work? What am I supposed to talk about?"

The answer is—anything you want! That's the beauty of talking to yourself. You can answer imaginary questions, prepare for a conversation with a native speaker, talk about your favorite hobbies, give a presentation to an imaginary crowd in your target language ... your possibilities are endless.

If you're an absolute beginner, you can start by training your mouth so that you're able to produce the sounds of your target language. You don't have to try to sound exactly like a native speaker, but it's crucial to learn how each letter sounds so that you can make yourself easily understood and avoid awkward sound-related mistakes.

You can check out Forvo to hear how native speakers pronounce words in your target language. Even if you can't find a word, you can add it, and most likely someone will record a pronunciation of it shortly. This can be useful whenever you come across a new word and don't know how to pronounce it. Simply listen to the recording and try to repeat the word until you can pronounce it correctly.

Once you're comfortable with the sounds and letters of your target language, you can take some time every day looking around your apartment, office, or whatever place you're in, and describe it, saying the names of the things around you out loud.

Another idea would be to talk about what you're doing right now. Are you walking your dog in the park? Are you cleaning the house? Are you cooking? Simply talk about what you're doing, what tools you're using, how long it takes, why you're doing it, etc. You can also chat about what you'll do next or what you want to do that day (which is a good way to introduce a future tense into your grammar!).

Speaking of introducing, why not introduce yourself? At some point you'll have to do this in your target language, especially if you schedule a conversation or a language exchange with a native speaker, so why not practice it with yourself beforehand? You can also imagine yourself going to a store to order something and recreate that small dialogue in your target language.

If you dedicate at least a few minutes to talk to yourself in your target language every day, you'll always have a way to find the words and phrases you want to learn next. After all, you want to keep learning and growing your vocabulary, right?

If you're an intermediate or advanced learner, one effective idea is to tell personal stories from your own life and what you've learned from each story. These can be:

- a past job rejection
- an important decision you made at some point in your life
- an uncomfortable situation that turned out to be a blessing
- a memorable argument you lost and what might have happened if you'd won (this is a nice way to master conditionals)
- a lovely moment you spent with your family
- an event that made you reshape the way you think.

Here's the bottom line: *The more emotional your story is, the faster it'll help you accumulate new words and phrases in your target language and make them stick.*

According to a series of studies, emotion can positively affect the encoding of information into your short- or even long-term memory. After all, you're sharing something really personal, something that means a lot to you, so even foreign language words can carry a strong meaning!

You never know when these stories might come in handy; maybe you'll share one of them with a native speaker. Even if this never happens, you'll have learned a lot in the language.

Another idea would be simply to express your opinion about a certain topic. You can talk about your views on a controversial topic, current affairs, politics, religion, etc. Just imagine you're having that conversation with a native speaker of the language.

If you already use some form of self-talk in your own language—to motivate yourself or cheer yourself up, for example—why not start doing it in your target language? That way you're taking an already formed habit and simply changing the language, thus making it a part of your daily life.

Whenever you run out of things to talk about, you can either take your last conversation in your native language and try to replay it in your target language, or simply try to summarize a book, movie, or video you enjoyed.

Alternatively, you can use ESL Discussions to locate with a new topic. That's not all though. Since you're alone and talking to yourself about anything you want, you can try to make it as fun as possible. Here's a way to do this: if you're like me, you might enjoy acting out imaginary arguments while in the shower, and of course, winning them. It takes showering to a whole new level!

Why not do the same in your target language? You can kill two birds with one stone: winning your arguments and using your target language. Try memorizing one or more new phrases before getting in the shower and start from there to show how good you are at winning arguments, no matter the language.

Just remember, you don't need to be fluent in a language to start speaking to yourself. Heck, you don't even have to know half the words, or even grammar, for the things you want to talk about!

Talking to yourself isn't an exam. It's a journey of curiosity, doubt, discovery, repetition, and small victories.

You might want to keep it a secret, though, if you feel people will think you're crazy, talking to yourself. You can leave them wondering how you speak your target language so well without talking to anyone!

Recording yourself is also very useful because you can listen to your voice afterwards and compare it to the original phrase. I recommend that you record phrases you find online in, say, podcasts or videos on YouTube, so that you can compare your accent to that of a native speaker.

Talking to yourself comes in handy when you find yourself at home and you want to describe your feelings today, or the things around you, or how your day was. It especially comes in handy when you're cleaning the house or doing any other daily, boring chores. All these tasks require little thought, so you can easily do them while practicing your target language alone. That makes you better in the language and the tasks more quickly and easily done! Win-win!

THE PHONE TRICK

No matter how much you talk to yourself and how much better and more fluent you think you've become, whenever you find yourself in public situations, all that skill that gave you confidence is gone. Vanished into thin air. Just like that. Poof!

So maybe talking to yourself isn't enough after all, if your goal is to achieve fluency. You've practiced and you feel very comfortable when speaking alone (to yourself), which makes your language skills seem to be way better than they really are. It turns out that if you want to get better at a language, you'll have to practice with other people at some point.

Chances are, you dread that situation.

Every interaction with other people in your target language feels like an exam. You feel so uneasy that your language skills narrow down to "*Ich heisse Kartoffel*" ("My name is potato")—if you can utter any words at all.

Why does this happen? Don't you feel very comfortable and fluent whenever you speak to yourself in your target language? Why isn't it the same in public?

Talking to yourself and talking in public are two very different situations. In the latter, other people come into play, so fear of judgment creeps in, sabotaging your language skills. This made me wonder, "Is there any acceptable way of talking to myself in public?"

Fortunately, yes, there is!

It's what I call "the Phone Trick," for lack of a better name, and it's one of my favorites that will bring lasting benefits to your language skills. It's the most acceptable way of talking to yourself in public with no one around you thinking you're crazy.

Let's see how it works.

- Go to a public place.
- Switch your phone to silent, so that you won't receive any unexpected call, and then pretend you're calling somebody or somebody is calling you. That "somebody" is an imaginary friend who speaks your target language, so your "conversation" will be in that language.
- You can either use whatever phrases you know in your target language or prepare a script in advance, creating a dialogue with your imaginary friend. That way you can put all your newly learned words and phrases into practice ... in public.

Simple, isn't it? The first few times you do this in public will be awkward, especially if you're on the shy side. The first time I did it, I had sweaty palms and an alarmingly fast heart rate, but it was worth it. "Practice makes perfect" holds true in this case. Believe me, this can do wonders—as long as you don't forget to switch your phone to silent.

Let me give you an example of a fake phone call.

You: "Hey, how are you doing?"

Sacred Pause (have a moment of silence while your "friend" talks to you, and think about what you'll say next).

You: "Great, thanks, I'm on the train back home right now. Did you talk to her?"

Sacred Pause (have another moment of silence, thus more time to create the next phrases in your head).

You: "Oh, cool. I thought you never would. I'm so happy for you. Where are you right now?"

Sacred Pause (take that awesome pause again, the one you wish you had every time you talked to native speakers of your target language).

You: "Oh, I see. Anyway, we'll see each other on Saturday, so we'll talk about it more then. Okay? See you Saturday. Bye!"

This was a rather simple example, so you can obviously enhance it with words and phrases about anything you want. No one can listen to what your imaginary friend is telling you on the phone, so your conversation might as well be about drawing unicorns, the last elections, or assembling turbomachines, for example. You can choose any topic you want and use any phrases you want to master, such as those you most recently learned.

Faking a call with an imaginary native speaker in public may sound like the craziest thing ever, but it can bring enormous benefits to your language learning skills. Why is it that? What's the best thing about this method? If there are native speakers of your target language around, they might strike up a conversation with you in that language! This saves you of the dreadful task of having to start a conversation with another person—in a foreign language. Others do it for you.

This has happened to me many times.

For example, I was at the Budapest airport and found out that my flight would be an hour late, so I sat down and grabbed my book, patiently waiting for my flight. Sitting beside me was a woman reading a newspaper in Spanish. Such a perfect opportunity to pick up my phone and fake a call with my imaginary Spanish friend, right?

That's exactly what I did, and it worked perfectly. Not only did I practice the language again, but after I "hung up," the woman immediately started talking to me in Spanish, telling me her flight was also late, which meant she had all the time in the world to have a nice conversation with me.

We chatted for half an hour in Spanish, only stopping because her flight arrived so she had to go. How's that for a nice, free, thirty-minute Spanish session? Also, I wasn't the one who took the first step—she did! All I did was trick her into taking it.

This is just an example of the benefits of this trick. But wait, there's more:

- By speaking in public, you expose your language skills to other people. They might not initially understand what you're talking about, but this trick helps you gradually become familiar with speaking the language when other people are around, which makes you more comfortable speaking in public.
- You can use any new word or phrase you want. You can prepare a script in advance and use all the new words and phrases you recently learned. The others can't hear your imaginary friend on the phone, so you might be talking about anything in the world. Take advantage of this and use that word you learned for, say, "side effects" of a medicine. You can do that anytime, anywhere.
- You can sound fluent and use everyday slang and phrases. You can pretend you've always known a language and come off as fluent in it in public. You feed the "fake it till you make it" mentality, and you reap the emotional benefits of being fluent

in your target language. This can be quite a motivator to keep practicing and becoming better.
- You can repeat the same dialogue over and over again. Change trains, go to the library, or get out of your office. Modifying your location allows you to use the same conversation all over again, thus strengthening those phrases in your mind.

For these reasons, the phone trick is one of my favorite ways to become better at a language. It's helped me increase my speaking speed, sound more natural in public, memorize new words and phrases, start conversations with native speakers, and meet new people who speak the language, all in one.

I keep using it, practicing, becoming better at it, making up more realistic, lively conversations, and enjoying every second. It'll feel awkward at first, and you might forget to switch your phone to silent or feel uneasy, but trust me: it gets better, and most importantly, you get better. Pick up your phone! I'm calling you in Spanish!

HOW ABOUT A VIDEO?

If you want to take your speaking skills to the next level, record yourself on video speaking your target language. Use your computer's webcam, a video camera, or a phone and start talking about anything you want. This method isn't as easy as talking to yourself, as the camera puts extra pressure on you.

You can take advantage of that, though, as you'll gradually learn how to speak under pressure and get used to it. This skill will come in handy as soon as you start having conversations with native speakers, which is another environment where you'll feel pressure.

Make videos of yourself daily, weekly, or monthly, and compare them to see how your speaking skills have improved with time. I recommend you do this weekly or twice a month, rather than every day, so that it's easier for you to notice how much you've improved.

If you want to take it a step farther, you can upload the videos to YouTube or Facebook so that you get feedback from native speakers. That way you'll also make sure you don't lose these videos, and you'll be able to see how much you've improved anytime, anywhere.

LEARN FILLER WORDS

When having a conversation with a native speaker, it's normal to get stuck at times, thinking of what to say next. If you get stuck too often, though, that can take a toll on your confidence and affect your speaking skills for the rest of the conversation.

This is where filler words in your target language come into play.

Filler words are words you also use in your native language that fill the gaps in your conversations while you think of what to say next. Consider these examples of filler words: *you know, pretty much, well, I'd say.*

Using filler words during a conversation can help keep your momentum going and boost your confidence because you won't stop speaking *and* you'll have time to think of what to say next. You'll also subconsciously help the other person give you time to think of what to say because the filler words close the gap that person might try to fill in the conversation.

Try to use some of these words in your next conversation, making sure you pick just one or two filler words to use. You wouldn't want to spend extra time trying to remember the filler words as you think of what you really want to say!

Speaking in your target language means you'll use a key ingredient in practice. That key ingredient is …

PRONUNCIATION

Some say it's impossible to acquire a perfect accent in a foreign language because you didn't learn it as a baby like you did with your own language. Trying to make it perfect so that you sound exactly like a native speaker isn't necessary. After all, you don't want to become a spy; you just want to learn a new language.

Some go farther and say you don't even have to try to improve your accent, as long as you learn how to pronounce the new letters and try to find sounds in your own language that are as close as possible to the sounds you hear.

After all, you have so many new things to learn in a foreign language—vocabulary, grammar, expressions, possibly irregular verbs, exceptions—why add pronunciation to the whole package?

I'm not objective when it comes to the importance of pronunciation, as it happens to be the thing that draws me to foreign languages the most. While the different way of thinking and words themselves attract me to languages, pronunciation is what makes me fall in love with them.

I've always loved music and sounds. I'd sit under a tree and spend time listening to the sounds of nature. I'd try to imitate sounds of animals or the funny voices of some of my teachers back in high school. I've always loved tuning my ear to the sounds around me. One could say that listening is my favorite skill, but just listening to the sounds didn't cut it for me. I wanted more. There were sounds I liked so much I wanted to imitate them right away, to make them mine.

That's exactly what happens with languages. I tune my ear to the new sounds, and if I like what I hear and imagine myself imitating those sounds perfectly and making them mine, that's what ultimately makes me fall in love with a language and try to make it mine. When I savor the sounds of a language, I try to practice my mouth and tongue movements so that I can imitate them comfortably.

We've previously discussed finding your own personal reasons *why* you want to learn a language. For me, being able to pronounce it exactly as I hear it is one of those reasons—even if I hardly ever reach a point where I can sound exactly like a native speaker.

Every language has its own melody, own pace, and unique word flow. The more time you spend listening and paying attention to the sounds of a foreign language, the more you get used to it and it becomes natural for you to incorporate things you hear into your way of speaking it.

From the moment we're born and as we grow up, we're exposed to the melody of our own language. We're not even aware of the fact that there might be another way to put words together—different types of melodies, sounds that can come from the human mouth that don't resemble the ones we already know. Because we don't know any different, we listen to the melody and sounds of our own language, and we gradually adopt them and use them in our own speech. At first, as babies, we find it hard to imitate all the sounds, but a moment comes when we can pronounce all the sounds of our language, and it's easy for others to understand what we say.

The big challenge is being able to do the same in the language you want to learn, to step out of the world of the sounds, the melody, the words and expressions you already know into another, different world—the world of the sounds of your target language.

You can find easier passages to that world if you identify what sounds the foreign language and your native language have in common and take advantage of the fact that you can already make those sounds.

As an adult, there are lots of shortcuts you can take to make language learning easier and more effective. That's something children don't have, which is why I strongly believe that it's easier to learn a new language as an adult than as a little kid.

How else can you improve pronunciation, and when should you try to do this during your language learning journey?

Generally, the earlier you decide to learn how to pronounce everything in your target language correctly, the better, because you won't have to unlearn things later on. Unlearning previous mistakes is usually a lot harder than learning new concepts.

So I recommend that you spend a few days just listening to the language, preferably before you start reading even basic words and phrases in it. After that, you can start learning your first words and how to pronounce them. This is a vital first step as it allows your mouth to get used to pronouncing things early on; as I mentioned, once you get used to pronouncing words wrong, it's harder to correct afterward.

But what if you're at a higher level than absolute beginner? What if you're already conversational in your target language? If you haven't taken that first step, then of course, all is not lost.

Let's see how you can improve your pronunciation at any stage of your language learning journey.

INITIAL STEPS

The first thing you can do to improve your pronunciation is ... *listen and observe.*

This is a subcategory of active listening, as we discussed in the "Listening" chapter. It's very important to pay attention to the sounds while listening—you're actively listening to understand what *sounds* are happening but not to understand the content of what's being said.

Don't turn webpages and other resources to a slow version of your target language. Expose yourself to the real speed of the language from early on. You can listen to online radio (TuneIn) or watch movies or videos on YouTube (preferably videos that have to do with something you enjoy—your favorite activities and hobbies, beauty tips, sports, anything you'd normally watch but in your target language).

Remember that the point here isn't to understand what the speaker is talking about, but to observe the sounds.

How different are some sounds from your own? How's the intonation? Would you use a similar inflection in your language for questions? What makes that language sound exotic? Try to answer these questions using the power of observation.

If you do this every day, you'll gradually start getting used to the sounds and intonation of the language. It'll help you improve not only your pronunciation, but also your understanding of the language more easily.

You'll get used to whatever you find difficult in your target language, as long as you keep at it.

When I say that I recommend you learn correct pronunciation early on in your language journey, that means, apart from listening and observing, I encourage you to go through YouTube videos and listen to how each letter is pronounced, as well as how each letter is pronounced between certain other letters (for example, think of the different sounds of English letter g: the g in "game" doesn't sound the same as the g in "gem"). Try to imitate these sounds and don't worry if you don't sound exactly like the recordings. All you need for now is to make sounds near what you hear so that native speakers can more easily understand you.

Completing this task will get you started and set the foundations of your language skills. Now, let's take a look at what else you can do.

SHADOWING

Shadowing is one of the best ways to make sure you improve not only your pronunciation in your target language but also your intonation (to match that of native speakers).

It's the act of parroting what you hear. All you have to do is listen to a recorded version of someone talking in your new language and try to mimic what you hear exactly how you hear it. This may sound a bit ridiculous, but it's a very effective way of not only improving your pronunciation but also your listening skills, as your ear will get used to the new sounds and the speed at which native speakers speak the language, making it easier for you to understand what's going on.

Listen to someone speak, or watch a video in your target language, and after a couple seconds, repeat what you heard. Make sure you can hear both the speaker and yourself talk. Don't worry if you don't understand everything you repeat; comprehension isn't the point here, so don't read any transcripts or subtitles while you listen. What matters is getting used to the new sounds, rhythm, and intonation, gradually making it part of your own speech. Reading letters won't help you, especially if your native language and your target language share the same alphabets. Just listen and imitate. Also, make sure you don't use shadowing during conversations with people; just recordings, radio, podcasts, or videos!

To make shadowing more effective, instead of continuously listening and mimicking, you can choose just one or two phrases to mimic and record them. How do you choose what phrases to imitate?

You can choose any phrase to record and imitate, but it's most effective if you find a phrase you can see yourself using in the future. The best phrases for that are those you can use for many different topics and occasions.

For example, say you're watching a YouTube video in your target language with English subtitles (a documentary, for example, as these usually have subtitles in many languages). Suddenly, you come across a phrase saying, "I don't know what to do about that."

This is something you can say for a lot of things and in a lot of different situations, so it's useful. Let's record it!

Other potentially useful phrases include the following:

- "If I remember well ..."
- "It's easier said than done."
- "What did you do last weekend?"
- "Recent surveys show that this is true."
- "I'm very passionate about that, and I wouldn't give it up for anything" (that could be a job, your favorite hobby, language learning, etc.).

If you find something about your favorite hobby or something you think you can use to talk about other topics, then just go for it. Don't look for the perfect phrase. Just listen or watch a video, let the phrases come to you, and choose one or two to shadow.

If you find a phrase like "but making orange cake isn't as easy as it seems" and you don't enjoy cooking (let alone baking cakes), then by no means should you choose that phrase as you won't see yourself using it.

Once you've found the phrase(s) you want, record them using your phone, your computer's recording app, or a program like Audacity that lets you record sounds on your computer. Don't record the whole context where you found it, just the phrase you want to imitate.

After you record it, try to mimic it a couple times. This might take a while as your tongue stumbles, trying to make the new sounds, but once you can mimic the whole sentence, record yourself. Then compare the two recordings.

If you notice any differences, re-record yourself trying to correct these differences, or try again the next day. Once you record yourself the next day, compare today's recording with yesterday's and with the original recording of the native speaker. Repeat the process until what you say exactly matches what the native speaker says.

If a phrase is too fast for you to imitate, Audacity lets you play the recordings slower. You can start by trying to imitate the slow version, and once you get used to it, increase the speed until you can speak it at normal speed.

This may seem like a daunting task, but it can be a tremendous help as you get used to the new intonations and start sounding more like a native speaker, even if, once you're speaking in the language, you say things other than what you recorded.

Actively listening and then repeating what you hear is a powerful way to improve your accent. Combine this with daily exposure to the language, and you'll see your pronunciation skills skyrocket.

SHADOWING WITH MUSIC

Singing along to the lyrics of your favorite song in your target language can also count as shadowing, as long as you're trying to imitate the sounds exactly as the native speaker pronounces them. In this case, you can't imitate any special intonation, though, because the singer is just following the melody of the song, but you can still improve the way you imitate certain difficult sounds in your target language. Using music will probably make the whole exercise more pleasant, as it's easier to listen to a song over and over again.

Shadowing isn't the only thing you can do while listening to music though. Let's see what else you can do.

HOW TO IMPROVE YOUR ACCENT THROUGH MUSIC

Let's demonstrate how you can improve your pronunciation by listening to your favorite songs, step by step.

1. Listen to the song without looking at the lyrics. Do this at least once or twice, but as many times as you like beyond that.

2. Once you get used to the song, try singing along to whatever words you recognize. If, for example, the song has a catchy chorus you can imitate, do that.

3. Look up the lyrics and listen to the song while you follow the lyrics (don't sing along yet). Notice how much you recognized before you looked up the lyrics. Pay attention to how unfamiliar words sound. Look up any unknown words to see what they mean, or read the translated version of the lyrics if you can find it.

4. Listen to the song and sing along by looking at the lyrics. Isn't it easier to follow the lyrics without getting lost now?

5. (Optional) Look for the karaoke version of the song and sing! Don't you sound more natural singing that song than before?

Repeat this process for any song you like by listening to it many times on repeat.

FINDING A MODEL SPEAKER

As you expose yourself to your target language more and more, you may come across a recording of a native speaker speaking your target language with a voice that doesn't differ much from yours. This person might be the same gender and around the same age as you, or have a similar voice. Whenever you encounter such voices or interesting ways of pronouncing your target language, try to find out who that person is, where you can find more content from this person, and use him or her as your model speaker.

What does that mean? It means you should try to sound exactly like that person whenever you speak your target language. You can do this through shadowing or listening to more and more content from that person.

As soon as you find a model speaker, collect videos and interviews of them. For model singers, make new playlists featuring them. I've compiled a playlist on Spotify full of singers whose voices are similar to mine and who sing in my target language. That way I can imitate them, so that I can sound exactly like them.

If you happen to live in a certain region of the country in which your target language is spoken, you can find a neighbor, a colleague, or a friend and make this person your model speaker (That doesn't mean you should go around recording him or her, as it'd probably be unacceptable in most, if not all, cultures; just try to imitate the speaker). You can even introduce him or her to WhatsApp and send audio messages to each other; that way you can get some recordings peacefully!

I've done this for German, having found three model speakers and a model singer whose voices are similar to mine, and these people are the ones I mostly turn to whenever I want to improve my pronunciation. I look for interviews or songs to listen to more and more German as they speak it. Keep in mind, this technique doesn't work to improve your listening skills, as you'll want to listen to as many people as possible so that you can understand all possible ways your target language sounds. When you want to improve your pronunciation, however, having model speakers definitely helps a lot.

Why are they helpful? Because sometimes you learn how to pronounce certain things in your target language and develop a certain intonation, and when you come across people who pronounce these words that you've already learned differently from you, it can be overwhelming. If you have model speakers who are definitely native speakers of the language who don't speak an obscure dialect, you'll always have a reference point to follow, and you'll know whatever you've learned is right and you won't have to relearn things.

If you're interested in learning a certain accent or dialect of your target language, find a model speaker who speaks in that accent or dialect. Then you can make sure you have a reliable source to learn it and be consistent.

LEARNING TO PRONOUNCE WORDS CORRECTLY

As you browse the Internet in your target language, you might come across words you don't know how to pronounce. In that case, all isn't lost.

You can use Forvo, which (as we saw in the "Talking to Yourself" chapter) is a website where people can post words in any language and native speakers will pronounce them. All you have to do is type the word you want to learn how to pronounce, check whether there's a recording for it by a native speaker, and play that recording. If your word isn't in the database, you can just submit it and wait until a native speaker records a pronunciation of it. If you're learning a certain variation of a language, like Spanish from Spain, you can check out from which region the speaker comes and pick the recording that matches what you want to imitate. You can also find out how to pronounce certain letters or a string of letters by looking up recordings of words that have these letters.

If you want to have entire phrases pronounced by native speakers, you can opt for Rhinospike instead. Like Forvo, it lets you listen to recordings of native speakers, but this time you can ask native speakers to pronounce a whole sentence. This is useful if you want to use a sentence often and want to pronounce it exactly like native speakers do. It's also helpful if you're interested in the intonation of your target language and how people change their voices according to the sentence type (if it's a question, for example).

DON'T TAKE IT TO THE EXTREME! - THE ACCENT TRAP

Maybe you're crazy about pronouncing everything perfectly? Perhaps you want to mix into a group of Italians without anyone noticing you're not Italian, or you want to go somewhere by bus and pretend you're Korean and be as convincing as possible so that your mother-in-law, who's sitting opposite you, doesn't recognize you and start talking to you? Whatever your reasons are, please beware because there's a trap there.

The accent trap!

If you try too hard to sound exactly like, say, native French speakers, you might end up spending way too much time and energy trying to make your accent perfect so that French people don't start speaking English to you in Paris whenever you speak French to them (probably the best way of proving your accent in French is perfect).

That's not a problem if pronunciation is what you want to focus on, but if you also want to improve other language skills, it might delay the learning process. It might even make you want to give up the language entirely if you don't sound 100 percent perfect at all times—which is unfair.

Think of how easy it is for you to know whether someone speaking your first language is a foreigner. Even if that person makes all the sounds correctly and has perfect intonation, perfect flow, and perfect speed, it's easy to spot a certain pronunciation of some words—one slightly mispronounced sound or even tiny inflations in sentences that you know a native speaker wouldn't do. Even if almost everything sounds right but just one letter sounds foreign, you might start wondering where this person comes from.

Overcoming that stage as a language learner would take too much time and practice—way too much because you'd also have to learn how to keep having a perfect accent when emotions kick in, when you're afraid, angry, agitated, etc.

I'm guilty of this fallacy.

When I was learning Hungarian, I spent way too much time trying to sound exactly like Hungarians, but no matter how hard I tried, at some point during a conversation, Hungarians would realize I was a foreigner.

I'd become desperate, and I'd practice more, repeat more and more sentences, record sentences in the language and my own version and then compare each version … but at some point my Greek accent would slip in and give me away. As soon as I realized how much I was harming myself and hindering my own language journey (because I spent months and months working on my accent without learning anything new in Hungarian), I decided to finally compromise my initial goal:

I decided I'd try to sound like a native, but with a touch of Maria.

By letting a small part of myself find its way into my accent in Hungarian (and any other language I wanted to learn), I made the learning process a lot smoother and faster, without compromising my enthusiasm for learning how to imitate foreign sounds. I also satisfied my Greek accent's complaints and need to crawl back into my foreign language accent wherever it found cracks.

I'm not a native speaker of my target language, and I'm not a spy either. I'm Maria, and these tiny little Greek details of my accent are a part of myself, a part of my character, a touch or Maria.

Making this compromise has enabled me to feel that my target language is really mine. There's a personal touch in there, and I've learned to be proud of that!

So to any native speaker out there, I say, "That's the way your language sounds when I speak it. I'll do my best to imitate the sounds as you make them and to make you understand me effortlessly, but it won't always work, and that's fine."

In other words, I want to pronounce all the sounds flawlessly, but don't care too much if small details give me away as a foreigner.

Ever since I changed my accent goals, I've felt less frustrated. I spend less time working on or worrying about my accent, and I concentrate on other areas of my language without feeling I'm wasting too much time.

If you're fluent in your target language and your only goal is to sound exactly like a native speaker, then by all means go for it. There's no reason not to do so. The sky's the limit. But if you also want to concentrate on other areas of your target language, or if you struggle with perfectionism when it comes to pronunciation, you can reconsider your accent goal.

How do you know if you've reached your new goal?

People won't be able to tell where you come from, but they'll notice a slight accent or maybe a different intonation when you become very emotional. It's perfectly fine, and hey, it adds a personal touch to your language skills. You're speaking the target language, and you're showing the world that this language is yours! You don't have a "Greek" accent or an "American" accent or the accent that gives your home country away.

You have *your* accent. An accent that gives *you* away. An accent that says it's you who speaks that language.

How much more personal can it get?

Bottom line:

Early on, learn to pronounce things right. If you want to sound exactly like a native speaker, don't beat yourself up if you don't accomplish it. Strive for a near-native accent and embrace your personal touch. What's not to love about that?

You should be proud that you're not monolingual, that you're brave enough to learn a foreign language and speak it in a great, albeit not perfect, accent.

WRITING

While speaking is inevitably one of the most important language skills, writing is also very important and an integral part of communication, so many language learners focus on that. Not everyone wants to speak one's target language; some want to learn how to write in it, so that they can send letters, write diary entries and blog posts, send messages to their friends … and that's perfectly okay.

Let's not forget there's no universal language skill that every learner has to master. We're the leaders of our journeys, we're different, and it's up to us to decide what we want to learn and concentrate on.

The process of writing what you want to say pushes you to concentrate on every word of the sentence, especially if you write using a computer and happen to have a spellchecker in your target language.

The good part about writing is that it helps you test and correct yourself because you have to come up with sentences in your target language and you have all the time in the world to think about what to write. You have time to review your vocabulary, grammar, syntax, and punctuation. You have time to think about whether you've written something right or wrong or whether you used the right verb conjugation. If you were speaking instead of writing, doing that would hinder your speaking abilities and slow you down.

As you speak the language, you can make minor errors or use a wrong word or a wrong conjugation, etc. If you don't get corrected, you'll hardly notice your mistake as you're concentrating more on communicating with others.

When you write, however, you still have to produce words and sentences in another language, but you can keep it private. You don't have to be concerned that people will judge you, like you might feel when speaking. You can also take as much time as you want to apply newly learned words and phrases to use, unlike during an actual conversation when you don't have time to think about everything. It's the best of both worlds!

You can also write about anything at all and not care about the mistakes you may make. When you're done writing, you can have a native speaker (or even more than one) correct it for you using Italki Notebooks. It's great for putting newly learned words and phrases to use before speaking. Once you get the hang of it, you'll come up with new sentences easier, and this will also help you during your conversations in the language.

Writing is also great for finding words that you already know but can't use in a sentence. If you've memorized a list of isolated words (something I don't recommend) and don't know how to use them, then writing is the perfect way to learn how to do that.

So some of us want to learn how to write well in our target language. How do we go about it?

Just as with any other language skill, you can improve your writing skills … by writing more! But that's not enough. Writing more is one thing, but writing correct or better is another.

Of course, writing in your own language feels a lot easier and a lot less awkward compared to writing in your target language (This becomes obvious as soon as you start trying to put your thoughts into foreign words on a piece of paper or on your computer).

That's when you realize you're a lot less confident in your foreign language than what you previously thought when it comes every little aspect of grammar, vocabulary, and even punctuation. Is this how native speakers start a letter or a diary entry? Do they use semicolons like you do in English? Are you employing the correct tense for what you want to say?

For many people (myself included, until recently), improving your writing skills means having to write these long essays on uninteresting topics so that your teacher can review them, correct them, and send them back to you.

Fortunately, as with any other skill mentioned in this book (or anything mentioned in this book, for that matter), there's another way of going about it. In fact, there are plenty of ways of going about it. Let's find out!

WRITE STUFF

One simple way to improve your writing skills is to sit down and write about what you did today. No matter how uninteresting or unimportant you think it is, these were twenty-four hours of your life, so why not write about what you did?

That's also a great way to improve your grammar, as you have to mess with the past or the future tense, depending on what time of day you're writing your entry. If your day is over, you'll inevitably write about what you've already done, but if you write your entry in the morning, you'll write about what you want to do or what you plan to do. This is also a great way to learn new vocabulary about things you do in your life, so you know you'll use it a lot in your target language as well.

Let's not forget improving your writing skills means improving your vocabulary and grammar, which are two of the key ingredients of languages, as we've previously discussed. So by writing diary entries, you'll improve your grammar and vocabulary skills for actions you do in your daily life, which you'll inevitably talk about at some point, should you want to use your target language to speak to others.

WRITING COMMENTS

Most people wouldn't consider this to be "writing" in a foreign language per se, but it's a great exercise to use when you're ready to start writing in your target language and make it public. The main advantage is that your comment doesn't have to be long; even one sentence would do.

You can start writing comments under anything that interests you: a page on Facebook, a page in a blog in your target language, a video on YouTube, a Q&A site, anything like that would work. Try to use your newly gained skills that way.

FINDING A WRITING PARTNER

Although writing is typically a solitary activity, you may want to consider finding another learner of your target language so that you can both write in the language regularly, just like a conversation partner, as we saw in the chapter about Speaking. You can show each other what you've written and discuss any language-related doubts, mistakes, or writing style. This is a great way to hold each other accountable and keep going.

REWRITE IT!

If you want to improve your writing skills without having to start from scratch on a blank piece of paper, you can take an already written piece of work and change the necessary words so that you can write about what you want and make it your own. That piece of work could be a song you love, several sentences from an article or blog post you like, or even a comment you saw somewhere and enjoyed reading. That way you get premade sentence structures, and you force your brain to think about how you could change them in your target language to personalize them.

What you write might turn out to make little sense or sound plain weird, but it can also turn into something deep, depending on what you think and how you change it according to your interests. You can have a lot of fun and think in the new language! You don't have to check to make sure that everything is right as much as you would if you started from scratch. If you want to rewrite songs, you might want to find words that match the song's rhythm or rhyme with other words, which makes the whole process even more fun and challenging!

GETTING YOUR ESSAYS CORRECTED

Now, you might be wondering how you can be sure that what you've written is correct. After all, by learning for free, you have no teacher to correct your essays, right? So how do we go about it?

Fortunately, our favorite Place Where our New Language Lives has a solution for this. In fact, it has plenty of solutions for this, as always. There are automated script correctors as well as websites where you can post your piece of writing and native speakers will correct it for you.

Italki Notebooks is one of these websites. It lets you post your own sentences, essays, or small texts, and native speakers will correct them for you. In return, you can also correct a text in your mother tongue once in a while. It's an excellent website with a great community. Every time I used it, I got several full corrections from different people within a couple hours of writing my text—often even with explanations about grammar, word use, etc. Sometimes native speakers would even suggest more than one possible correct example or sentence.

As long as you get feedback about what you write and do something with that feedback, you're good. For example, apart from using the correct forms in future texts you write, you can make flashcards of expressions you got wrong or revise the specific grammar point you apparently struggled with during writing.

For single phrases or very short texts, you can also use HiNative. This website and app lets you ask native speakers anything about your target language. You can post phrases there and ask native speakers to correct them. You can also ask them if a phrase sounds natural, what's the difference between two words or phrases in your target language, and what different meanings a word can have. You can even ask them to give you examples of where you can use a specific word. All these make this app an excellent resource to improve not only your writing skills but also almost any language skill you want. Try it out to see what you can learn!

WRITING SUMMARIES

Another excellent way to improve your writing, as well as your vocabulary and grammar skills, is writing the summary of a book, article, or blog post you read or a movie or video you've watched. They don't have to be in your target language; you can summarize in your target language something you've read or watched in your native language. Say you want to explain what you've experienced to someone who only speaks your target language. How would you go about it?

This is an excellent exercise as it forces your brain to think of different words in your target language so that you can explain exactly what you experienced using fewer words. It puts your language skills to the test, and you might want to use what you end up writing for future reference, especially if you schedule a conversation in your target language and the topic will be about a great movie you've seen or book you've read, etc.

If you're reading a book in your native language, you can also comment on what you read in your target language. Read some pages, like you normally would, and then grab a piece of paper to comment on what caught your interest, what you read about today, something you liked, etc. Just make sure you make all these comments in your target language. You'll be surprised by how many new words and phrases you'll collect doing this activity.

START SMALL

If you've never written anything in your target language, instead of starting with a long essay or a diary entry, you could start by writing short, simple, informal pieces. It'll help you concentrate your writing on things you want to work on and keep you from getting discouraged. You can focus on only one topic at a time and get inspiration from the Place Where Our New Language Lives. You can also look for things to write about in your native language and then try to translate them to your target language. It's not bad to think big, but sometimes one must start small.

SHORT STORIES

Another cool way to improve both your writing and your vocabulary skills is writing short stories. They can be real, personal stories or pure fiction. They can be as short as a couple sentences or as long as you want.

Try to make up a short story in your new language by using all the new words you want to learn today. This will put your language skills to the test and will train your brain and your imagination, so that you can use them all effectively.

The story might end up being pretty weird, but the main point is to put everything you know into practice, make those new words stick, and get more comfortable writing in your new language. The weirder the story is, the more likely it is to stick to your brain and help you memorize all the new words and phrases you want to add—so let your imagination run wild. Anything can happen in your story, as long as you include the words you want to learn. If you're brave enough, you can share the short story online so that native speakers can correct poorly written parts or misspelt words. That way you'll make sure you know how to use your new words in context correctly so that you can use them in the future.

Even if you don't consider yourself a master in writing (or if you believe that you have no writing talent whatsoever), some daily scribbling can go a long way toward improving your language skills, even when you have to speak the language.

IMPROVING SPEAKING THROUGH WRITING

Writing and speaking have one thing in common: you're the one producing new words and sentences. You're not reading or listening to ready-made material. No wonder you can combine the two skills and speak the language through writing.

If you want to get better at speaking, you can choose to write conversational language rather than long sentences you'd only find in a book. Try to write as if you're talking, since it's highly likely you'll want to use what you write as prepared scripts for a speaking session. Try to keep it simple so that you know you'll be able to use such sentences orally.

You can also try texting people in your target language. One app that can help you do this is HelloTalk. Think of it as a messaging app like WhatsApp or Facebook Messenger but for language learning. It contains translation tools as well as correction tools (e.g., if you write a sentence with the wrong grammar, it autocorrects it and shows you your mistake). You can use the app to text native speakers in the language you're learning. If you find valuable vocabulary and sentences from the chat, you can use them to write a potential dialogue you might have with a speaking partner during a conversation.

You can also record and send voice messages, so if you're still looking to get in a bit of speaking practice, you can do that. Your HelloTalk profile also lets you record a voice message to introduce yourself, if you want.

Finally, you can post Moments in your target language and native speakers will correct them for you. These Moments are visible in the entire HelloTalk community, which is big, so native speakers can find you and correct any mistakes. You can also follow other people who post Moments in your target language. There's so much great learning material there, especially if you go to the "Learn" tab under "Moments."

BECOMING A POLYGLOT FOR FREE - STUDYING MORE THAN ONE LANGUAGE

Languages are like tattoos. Some say that as soon as you get one, you might start thinking about which one you'll get next.

Turns out that language learning is similar: as soon as you become conversational and create a solid foundation in one language (especially after doing so by using the mentality and methods described in this book), the first thing that comes to mind is *"Hey, that actually works. I can learn foreign languages! What should I learn next?"*

This is exactly the reason why many polyglots strive for "conversational" and not "complete" fluency. They find what works for them, the whole process becomes addictive, and they want to learn more and more languages using what they learned. This happens to me too; as soon as I become conversational in one language, I change my language project (but I still maintain and try to improve all my languages at the same time, while I concentrate on my main language project). I don't do that for every language I learn, though, as I want to master German. As we saw, the term "fluency" is pretty vague and can mean different things to different people.

If you're already thinking about your next language project and can't wait to get started with it, that's normal. As you keep learning languages, you'll realize it gets easier each time, no matter how hard the language you want to learn is, because you get used to the new mentality (as well as the language routine and your favorite methods), so you don't have to spend too much time figuring out whether you can learn a language as you already know the answer: why yes, of course I can!

There are some pitfalls to avoid though:

- Make sure you have a solid foundation in your first language before you start learning the next one. Otherwise, both languages will be hard to maintain, and you'll quickly forget what you've already learned.
- If the two languages belong to the same language family (like Spanish and Portuguese), make sure you're intermediate (or preferably upper intermediate) in one of them before you start learning the next one. Even if you think you won't, it's very easy to mix the two—trust me. Been there, failed that.
- Don't expect the same methods to work for all languages. Chances are they will, but if they don't, fear not; each language is different, and it's normal to change some methods from time to time, especially if the resources are more limited. Basque was my second language after Spanish, and I did have a hard time with that because Basque resources were rather limited in 2014, while Spanish ones were all over the place.
- Don't be afraid of trying something you'd previously rejected. You never know when it will come in handy. Also, don't forget that you change overtime. A method that you used to find fun might suddenly become boring. That's perfectly normal, and a clear indicator that you should try a different method.

As you learn more and more languages, you'll gradually get better at the whole process of learning a language, and you'll also get more confident in yourself and what you can do. Embarking on a new language learning journey, as well as maintaining it, will become easier, and it's highly likely you'll become addicted to the success that comes with perseverance. You'll want to add more and more languages to your collection, and thus gain access to more and more different worlds and cultures out there.

LINGUISTIC TERMS - DO I HAVE TO LEARN THEM?

You may be wondering, if we're the leaders of our journey and use online material, movies, music, and everything else we proposed to learn our target language, how do we learn what modal verbs are, what the gerund is, what the subjunctive mood is, and all those language terms in the new language?

If this is you, then I feel you. We've been taught all these things at school, so anyone learning a language has to know these terms to become fluent, right?

Wrong!

We don't all want to be academics and linguists. Some (if not most of us) just want to be able to communicate in the language, read our favorite books, watch our favorite movies, and travel to the country where the language is spoken and converse comfortably with native speakers.

So why do we need to know the names of each linguistic term? Past perfect continuous, future perfect, vernacular perfect but sometimes imperfect, relative clauses, passive voice, active voice, passive middle hyperactive voice ... (Yes, I love making up my own tenses and voices).

Now, you might be shaking your head, thinking Maria has no idea what she's talking about, especially if you're a language teacher. This is how you're supposed to learn a foreign language, make your journey easier, and ace any language exams!

Well, yes. But it's not for everyone. Let me give you a recent example.

I took the B1 exams in German after three months of studying the language on my own. (This was during the last time I tried to learn it, the one with a happy ending.) For those that don't know what the "B1" label means, it's lower intermediate at the Common European Framework levels. A1 and A2 are for beginners and upper beginners respectively, B1 and B2 for intermediate and upper intermediate learners, and C1, C2 for proficient learners.

As soon as I arrived at the institute where the exams would take place, I joined other learners who were talking about strong and weak objects in a sentence, or verbs that have strong and weak objects, or something like that. I'd no idea what all that was, so I just nodded along, pretending I understood. As time passed, they added more and more terms that were unknown to me, and I began to feel insecure.

"What on earth are they talking about? Am I supposed to know these things? Are we even taking the same exams? Did I come to a wrong exam?" I wondered as I sat there, watching them, completely confused, unable to say a thing.

After a while, I couldn't resist the temptation to ask if they could give me an example in the language of all the terms they were talking about. They struggled a bit to think of something, and then they came up with a phrase and shared it with me.

I don't remember what it was, but I remember breathing a sigh of relief. "Aaaah, that's what you're talking about? Thanks a lot, I was kinda lost," I confessed. I actually was familiar with what they were talking about; I knew how to use phrases like the one they shared, but I'd no idea what the terms were that described those phrases.

They all looked at me, surprised. "How come you don't know what these are? Are you sure you're taking the right exam?"

Oh boy, I'd asked myself the same question moments ago ... Well, I passed the exam—with excellent scores, I might add—despite not having a single idea of what those terms were. Even now that my level in German is higher, I still don't know.

I'm willing to guess most German native speakers don't know those terms either. In fact, I've witnessed quite a few cases where learners of a language would ask a native speaker to help them with, say, the modal verbs, only to be met with a blank stare—similar to mine when I heard those students in my B1 exam.

So what's going on? Are native speakers not fluent in their language because they don't know the terms? Did I not learn German correctly because I never learned any terms?

Absolutely not.

Granted, if you're a fan of terms and you want a name for every new piece of grammar you come across in your target language, there are still a lot of free resources out there that can help you. Google any grammar term you want to learn and see what appears. If you're not familiar with the names of the terms in your target language, write them in English and add the name of the language. You'll most likely find not only learning resources but also online exercises so that you can practice with the new material.

My point is that, terms or not, you can find anything you want out there for free. Choosing to learn those terms is entirely up to you. I don't do it, but maybe you want to because it helps you learn faster. None of us is right or wrong. We do what works best for us individually.

Think of your language learning journey as a garden that you decorate with ornaments. You can either pay for ready-made ornaments or make your own exactly as you want them. The ornaments are the language learning material and methods you use, and the garden is your own way of learning.

The most important part is to work on your garden. Make sure you follow a routine to care for it, and—according to your needs at any given time—you add or remove the ornaments you want.

STUDYING FOR A LANGUAGE CERTIFICATE

What if you want to get a certificate in your target language? Maybe you want to get a better job, or you just want a piece of paper with your name on it to remind you of all the effort and hours you've put in to reach a certain level in your target language?

If you're interested in preparing for a language certificate (for whatever reasons), fear not; preparing for it without having to pay for books, teachers, or courses is possible. How?

The best thing you can do is thoroughly study the exam that interests you. What is it about? How long does it take? What kind of exercises do you have to expect? What topics do you have to study?

Always look for free past papers of the exams you want to take. If you find any past papers online, study them thoroughly, and try to do a mock exam in real time using them. (Don't forget to time yourself while you do that.) To find past papers, google the name of the exam (or the university that offers it) and add "past papers" or "practice tests" next to it (e.g., "GOETHE C1 past papers"). Alternatively, you can look for practice tests and see what you can find.

It's important to do this because you're trying to figure out what the examiners expect of you, what they will test you on. They don't expect you to know absolutely everything about a language, even if you want to get the highest certificate there is. I got the Certificate of Proficiency in English from two different universities, but I also recognize I was far from fluent in English at the time. I just knew what to study and what to expect, so I succeeded.

You see, getting a certificate and becoming fluent in a language are two different things. In the first case, you're very good at doing what the examiners expect of you. You can find out how to ace those exams through practice. We've already discussed the second case; the definition of fluency differs, depending on who you ask.

As you keep looking for past papers and practice tests, you'll notice common patterns. The more you study, the better you'll know what topics they usually have texts about, what kind of vocabulary you should work on, what topics you have to prepare for in advance of the oral exams, and what essays you have to expect. Try to look for past papers with model answers so that you can test yourself and know how to respond to each exercise and question. Cover the answers, set the timer, and test yourself using the past papers.

Chances are, you'll also find relevant YouTube videos about the exam you're interested in. Start your search with the name of the exam (e.g., "Spanish DELE B2") and add "tips" or "sample exam." You can find videos with tips on what to expect, what to watch out for, what to focus on, and how the exams are carried out. You can even find sample oral exams to get a better picture of what to expect during a speaking exam.

If you can't find more than one or two sets of past papers or practice tests, don't worry. Just make sure you know how long the exams last and what they'll test you on. If there are different tests within the exam—like reading, listening, speaking, and writing—here's what you can do to prepare for them:

First, identify which one of them you think is your biggest weakness, and work on this first.

To prepare for the reading part, read online newspapers and articles about different topics (science, technology, nutrition, current affairs, etc.) every day. You can also use any of the methods from the "Reading" chapter under Section 2.

For listening, make sure you don't use headphones, as the sound is too clear compared to what you'll most likely face during your listening exams. Instead, use your computer's speakers; and if you have a laptop, try going to different environments to practice listening, so that you're better prepared to face any type of conditions during your listening exam.

For writing, look up any possible topics you may have to deal with, write essays on them, and have native speakers on Italki correct them, as we discussed in the "Writing" chapter under Section 2.

Finally, for speaking, you can watch some sample speaking exams on YouTube to get a better picture of what the exam will be like. Type the name of your exam on YouTube and look for sample speaking exams. Just like with writing, you can look up what kinds of topics you'll most likely have to deal with and practice them, using any of the methods we discussed in the "Speaking" chapter under Section 2.

Even though I'm not a fan of language certificates, I still sit some exams now and then. So far, I've passed them all successfully, even though I almost always opt for intermediate-level exams, not the most advanced ones. I typically research what they expect of me and what they usually ask for so that I can prepare myself as much as possible before each exam. I do all these for free. I don't even buy any "preparation for X exam" books. There's so much advice and useful content, as well as so many placement tests online that I've never needed to buy any book or course to get the certificates I want. I'm taking my first advanced (C1) exam this year, and I'm using exactly what I'm proposing here.

If all this doesn't seem enough to you and you want to feel fully prepared for a language certificate, then you can opt for a book with practice tests or past papers. Yet, in that case make sure it also has answers somewhere, so that you can test and correct yourself.

Because the exams themselves cost money, getting a language certificate is never free, so you may not want to risk failing an exam because you feel you didn't prepare for it as much as you could. In this instance, if you can't find much free content online, you can opt for a book with practice tests and past papers. I choose to take that risk—to take the exam—because I don't want to breach my "Zero-Euro Policy" (my personal policy of paying zero euros for learning), but you don't have to do that. Remember: learning a language and getting a language certificate are two different things.

DID YOU FIND ANY COOL RESOURCE THAT'S NOT IN THIS BOOK?

If you found a great free language learning resource and want to share it with other people so that you can help them, please feel free to join and share it in my Facebook group "Fluent For Free - How to learn languages without spending a dime," or send me an email at maria@fluentforfree.com so that I can add it to my website fluentforfree.com. Let's create the biggest free language resources database for everyone to enjoy! Let's spread the message that free language learning is possible—and fun! Who knows, maybe a lot more lives can be saved that way? :)

If you need links to any of the resources mentioned in this book, please visit fluentforfree.com/links.

This section might have completely overwhelmed you, as there are a lot of materials and methods suggested, but the point isn't to read and implement everything all at once. You can come back and reread sections of interest anytime you want and as often as you need. You'll also want to go back after you're done reading the next section, which talks about how to make use of all these methods, choose what works best for you, and come up with a language learning plan that will lead you to success.

SECTION 3

Becoming The Leader - Creating A Language Routine

"Excellence is an art won by training and habituation."

—Aristotle

So far we've talked about setting our personal language goals and we've looked at what free material is available out there and how we can make the most of it.

This is, however, not all it takes to become successful at learning a language. You can use the best methods or learning material in the world, but that alone does not guarantee success.

You also have to become the leader of your language journey. This means you have to integrate everything you've learned so far and turn it into an efficient learning routine—a routine you can follow by spending as little as thirty minutes of your time per day—that will lead you to success..

In this section, you'll learn how to create a plan that works for you and how to make sure you'll follow it, so that giving up will never be an option again.

You'll learn:

- How to make the most of the time you spend learning a language
- How to choose the methods that work best for you
- How to create your language routine and make sure you stick to it

Let's dive right in!

CHOOSING THE METHODS

By now you've come across way too many methods and suggestions. It turns out that there are too many free methods and resources out there!

The good thing is that you don't have to use or even try them all to become fluent. As we previously discussed, all you have to do is choose some methods and combine them.

How do you know which ones to choose, though, so that you don't waste too much of your time trying everything?

Let's look at some basic criteria that can help you.

A suitable method must:

- Be enjoyable: if you don't have fun with it, it will be hard to stick to it every day. If a method makes you feel good, you'll want to use it again and again because you find it pleasant.
- Be relevant to you: even if it doesn't involve your interests directly, you'll want to learn words and phrases that you'll most likely use. I don't think you'd stick to a method that teaches you all the colors, animals, or furniture first, when none of this is urgent or interesting for you to learn. Instead, focus on a method that satisfies your language learning goals.
- Help you get better in your target language: even if it's enjoyable and relevant to you, if it doesn't help you learn more, it's not suitable. This can be tricky, though, because you can't tell

whether you're becoming better at the language overnight; you have to allow one week or more to see if the method truly helps you. Don't worry; it won't be hard for you to use a method for a week or more if you have fun with it and it's relevant to you.

A method has to be fun and relevant to you, and it has to help you become better at your target language. That's what matters. Even if you find a method that teaches you the supreme past perfect perpendicular in four seconds, it doesn't mean it's perfect for you. This is the criteria someone else thought you should learn (For the record, there's no such tense in any language anyway).

Choosing methods is all about you. You're the leader; you're the learner; you know what's best for you, and, through trial and error, you decide. Never mind what everyone else says.

- Do you find it fun?
- Is it relevant to you?
- Does it help you get better in the language?

If the answer to all three questions is yes, then congratulations! You found a method that works for you!

Of course, seeing whether a method fulfils the criteria we've proposed might also take time. If you ask any successful language learner, they'll probably tell you they had to change methods at some point, or they didn't find the methods that were perfect for them right away. You shouldn't worry too much about the whole process.

Always remember: You're not trying to find the right way of learning languages; there isn't any. You're trying to find what works for you and pushes you to use it more and more. That's not the right way of learning—it's your way of learning. It's that one word, "your," that makes all the difference.

You're looking for a combination of methods. Following several methods (or even just a few) that supplement each other is more effective than following just one and becoming a slave to it.

Why is this important? Let me explain.

Even if the methods I used were actually working for me, as soon as I stopped having fun with them, I switched to other methods. If they were fun but weren't really helping me improve my language skills, I'd either stop using them altogether or just use them during my free time, not the time I dedicated to language learning.

Duolingo, which I discovered during its first year of operation, was one of the reasons I decided to finally start learning Spanish. The first option was Spanish, so I chose Spanish and tried Duolingo to see if it delivered what it promised.

During the first weeks, I was completely in love with Duolingo, and I'd use it every single day without a pause. To this day I credit Duolingo for helping me understand the importance of doing something every day to learn a language.

As the days passed, though, I realized that, while I had fun with the website and I used it every day, I wasn't making that much progress in the language. I was just happy because I'd achieved that feeling of accomplishment Duolingo gives you when you complete one part of your Language Tree.

I wasn't able to pick the phrases that were more relevant to me and focus on them; I also had to learn the names of animals, colors, and furniture, even though I saw no use in learning all those from early on.

At the same time, however, Duolingo did help me learn some basic phrases that were relevant to me, so I decided not to give up on it completely. I just started supplementing it with other methods. For example, back then Duolingo taught no grammar whatsoever, and I wanted to learn how to conjugate certain verbs. So I started using an online verb conjugator in the way I explained in the "Grammar" chapter under Section 2. So not only did I use more than one method, but I also made sure to use whatever part of each method would be immediately useful to me first.

Learn from my example, and don't be afraid of trying new methods or even ditching them if they no longer fulfill any of the criteria we discussed.

As long as:

- you learn every day,
- you put your needs first,
- you have fun learning the language and are hungry to learn more, and
- you keep going no matter what comes your way,

There's absolutely no way you won't learn a foreign language successfully.

Maybe you won't learn it as fast as you wanted to, but point 4, "keep going," will prevent you from stopping. As your needs in the language expand, so will your vocabulary and grammar skills.

Putting your own needs first is all-important. Don't fall into the trap of asking what you're supposed to learn next. Instead, ask what you want to learn next. Trust yourself, your needs, and what you want to say in the language, and go step by step; don't expect to learn everything at once—and keep going, no matter what comes your way.

If you follow all this advice, you'll not only learn a language more successfully and for free, but you'll also become a much better version of yourself because:

- You'll notice the wonders that come from doing something every day.

- You'll discover what you're capable of doing as long as you keep going no matter what.
- You'll improve your confidence as you realize you're perfectly capable of becoming better in the language and leading yourself to fluency and that you don't need anyone else for that.
- You'll eventually open up to more people as you look for ways to practice your target language. Not only will your language skills improve, but your conversational and approaching skills will too—trust me. I'm introverted, but I can transform into the most fun-loving, outgoing, conversational person as soon as I find the adequate circumstances to do so.

As we described when talking about the perfect method myth, if you can identify the methods you find most enjoyable and that give you the best results, jot them down on a piece of paper and hang it on your wall or somewhere that you can see it at all times. Build your own set of methods for your own success, which will be perfectly tailored to you and your needs.

If some polyglots and successful language learners follow a method you don't find enjoyable or that doesn't work for you, please feel free to ditch it and use other methods.

The methods that successful language learners use may inspire you and make you want to try them out, but you have to feel free to stop using them if they don't cover the criteria we discussed. You shouldn't feel bad about yourself because they don't work for you. That doesn't mean you're not fit for language learning; it means you haven't found what's best for you yet. Please do not fall into the trap of comparing yourself to others; many unknown factors are at play, so it's an unfair comparison from the start. For example, what if that successful language learner is rich and able to spend a lot of time learning a language? What if they can afford to travel to the country where people speak that language? What if their mother tongue or a language they know already is very close to that language they learned? These are some of the factors that can come into play, which is why comparing yourself to anyone else does nothing but make you miserable.

You want to compare yourself to you—not others.

So once you're happy with a set of methods, you can either make yourself a study plan to keep yourself accountable, or you can use your method combination every day.

If you're an absolute beginner in the language, follow the same criteria, but start with a dedicated free language learning platform to learn the basics first. Google "X free lessons for beginners," where X is your target language, and see what online platforms you can find. Alternatively, you can use Duolingo if it offers a course in your target language, and gradually supplement it with other methods or media as you learn the basics.

Let's see what you can do next.

CREATING A LANGUAGE LEARNING PLAN

For as long as I can remember, I was always more practical and preferred the logical side of things. I was good at math and science but not so skilled at history or literature.

So naturally, when I got around to teaching myself languages, I went for a more practical approach to the whole procedure. Rather than thinking of terms and conjugations and tables and all those boring things I associated with languages.

Eventually, I created with the following plan:

Effective language learning is all about:

- Collecting language material that's relevant to you
- Learning this language material using your own favorite methods
- Putting your new knowledge to use to make it stick for good, and having fun doing so

At school, we didn't have to collect any language learning material. Others had already done this for us, mainly teachers and their textbooks. They also decided what method we should follow, which meant either repeating phrases or studying certain words and phrases on which we'd be tested the following day. We'd put our new knowledge to use by trying to write essays in the language, and the teacher would collect them to correct them. At times, we'd even speak about a certain topic chosen by our teachers or our textbooks.

But, as you've probably guessed by now, there are infinite ways to approach these three stages of language learning.

Every person is different. We all have our own preferences, our own hobbies, and our own goals for our target language. If you love basketball and want to learn English so that you can watch NBA games, you'll collect basketball-related language learning material, watch NBA matches online, and try to collect new basketball terms and phrases people use from there. You'll choose any method(s) from what we proposed in Section 2 to learn these new phrases, and you'll put your knowledge to use by chatting online with American NBA fans, or using the live chat next to the games you watch online to analyze what happened during each game. That way you can make the whole language journey relevant to you and make sure you have fun in the process.

How many times has someone told you, "I learned X language because I played computer games in it"? They accomplished this by using material that was relevant, immersing in it daily, and having fun in the process!

As soon as you start associating the foreign language with just another way of talking or writing about your favorite things and concerns—and not another subject with grades, tests, and exams—then you can make language learning a lot less boring and more of what it deserves to be: fun and rewarding.

Try to focus on results, not time. Instead of saying, "I'll spend thirty minutes learning my language," say "I'll revise ten phrases today" or "I'll collect five more phrases" or "I'll have a conversation." Measuring results is more effective than measuring time.

Keep your active study sessions short so that you can maintain focus and not become overwhelmed. Thirty minutes a day or fifteen minutes twice to three times a day are good examples. You're after regular revision and repetition. You don't really need to spend more time daily unless you're very serious about the language and know you can follow this long term. Smaller chunks of time are more doable, as you won't need as much motivation to spend fifteen minutes on a language as you'd need for an hour or more. Short sessions are also easier to fit into your daily schedule.

I also recommend finding a fixed time during the day to dedicate to your active study sessions. This can be right after you wake up, right before you go to sleep, or during dead times you regularly have during the day, like while you're on the bus or waiting somewhere.

During your active study sessions, you can opt for a dedicated free language course and use any extra time you find for media and other resources.

Make sure that not everything you do involves studying the language. Spend some time exposing yourself to the language and having fun with it! For example, you can listen to a podcast in the language while you drive to work, watch a movie and turn the language to the target language, listen to some music, read a book, or watch videos. Pay attention to what you do during the day that involves using your language, and try to replace the language with the one you're learning, whenever possible.

Doing things you normally wouldn't do because of language learning doesn't make much sense. If you don't watch videos in your native language, don't do it for the language you're learning. If you don't like blogs, don't start reading blogs because they're in your target language. Language learning has to fit into your lifestyle, not the opposite.

These are not active study sessions, but they will make sure you don't skip the fun part of learning a language and they'll maintain your motivation to add more active study sessions to your life.

For example, this is what I do in a typical day:

- Wake up
- Have breakfast while listening to the radio
- Wait for the bus while listening to music
- Read on my Kindle while on the way to work
- Go on Facebook to catch up with friends and read interesting articles
- Watch a movie or read more
- Go to bed

Notice how many tasks I can do in the language I want to learn:

- I can listen to the radio in German.
- I can listen to music in German.
- I can read content in German on my Kindle.
- I can go on Facebook (which I have set to German) and read interesting articles in German.
- I can watch a movie or read more in German.
- Although I can't sleep in German, all the rest are things I normally do, so I don't change my daily life for languages; I just change the language and that's does the trick. I don't even have to find extra time for language learning!

This little change also prompts me to add more active study sessions to my life because I don't always understand what's happening on the radio, podcasts, music, or books when they're in German, which pushes me to study more so that I can understand them.

Even if your schedule is very different every day, you can most definitely spend some time doing language-related activities during the day. Identify them and turn them into your target language (as long as you can find free materials for them).

I know that I've shown you way too many methods, but try to focus on no more than two or three at a time so that you won't become overwhelmed and spend too much time trying methods instead of learning. Keeping the whole process simple is vital.

BREAKING BIG TASKS INTO SMALLER

Often language learning seems too big of a task. As you've probably realized by now, language learning isn't something you can do in a few weeks or without effort. It's a hard process, with ups and downs, embarrassing mistakes, yet small victories too.

When you're about to start learning a language, it's natural to think of what lies ahead, which might feel overwhelming. It's a whole new language, a whole new set of words and grammar rules other people spent years or even a lifetime to learn. All that seems (and is) too much.

So how can you avoid becoming too overwhelmed by our language learning journey?

You can break a big task into smaller, more manageable ones.

You've probably seen some artists draw small squares on a photo so that they can paint it. My grandfather used to do that all the time. I'd find photos of landscapes divided into tiny squares all over the place. As a kid, I wondered why on earth he'd spend so much time using his ruler and pencil, trying to divide the picture into so many squares of equal size so that he could paint it. Why was that necessary? Why didn't he just paint that picture? He even drew squares on his canvas!

For years I never asked him why he did it. I just assumed it made it easier for him to calculate the distance between every object that was in the photo.

One day, years later, it hit me. He was actually breaking the big task of painting a photo into smaller tasks! It was way easier to paint the photo that way, and it was indeed easier to calculate the distance between objects too.

Of course, my grandpa also knew how to paint. But theoretically, if one breaks a painting down into tiny squares and starts coloring each square, they can paint it, even with little to no skill. After all, anyone can paint a tiny little square, say, black, right? It doesn't require too much talent or knowledge, other than probably a steady hand.

That's how it also works with language learning. You can take that huge task and start breaking it into smaller ones—as small as you consider manageable. There's no rule to that.

Every journey begins with a small step!

Each time you master one of these small tasks will be a small victory that will bring you joy and further motivation to keep going. And as you maintain your motivation and keep going, you'll eventually complete all the small tasks, which together make up the bigger one.

Sounds obvious, doesn't it?

Yet by using this simple technique, you can manage to learn not only a language (no matter how hard or how foreign it is to you), you can also learn any other skills you want.

By choosing to break down any new term in your target language (be it a new, weird sentence syntax, a crazy-sounding conjugation, a word you can't remember, etc.), as long as you break it into smaller tasks and work on those tasks one by one, you can learn it.

Who decides how small these tasks can be? You do—according to what you consider manageable. My grandfather used to draw squares to paint, but my squares would definitely have to be smaller than his to do that, as my painting skills aren't as good as his. It's up to you—what you can manage, the time you want to spend on a task, your attention span, etc.

So the next time you come across a language-related task that seems long and daunting, chunk it up! Make a marginal adjustment to your routine.

Break this big, ambitious goal of becoming fluent in a language down into these more manageable decisions, the decisions you have to make correctly along the way to improve the odds of achieving the outcome you desire.

Success is all about these tiny little decisions: Deciding to sit at your desk and put in just a little extra time at the end of the day before you go to bed. Choosing to turn off the TV, put your remote control down, and study your dream language instead, if only for a few minutes every day.

Let's see how you can break big tasks into smaller ones in practice, and why I insist on doing something every day.

THE POWER OF DOING SOMETHING EVERY DAY

One day, during my daily jogging routine, I started thinking about the skills I've gained thanks to language learning. Languages have changed my life in ways I never expected they would, so I tried to narrow down the skills to the ones that have helped me the most in my language journey.

After a couple minutes of heavy thinking and running, I realized I could narrow them down to just one. One skill to rule them all. If you want to learn languages effectively, the number one skill you must possess is self-discipline, or as I call it, The Power of Doing Something Every Day.

I can't tell you how much this has helped me, not only with languages, but in every aspect of my life. The small task of doing something every day and sticking to it can do wonders and move mountains, so much so that I've applied it to anything else I want to get better at, be it health, fitness, music, reading books, learning new things, researching—anything. It always works!

Let's see how you can go about it.

- Choose what part of the day you'll dedicate to studying your target language. It can be early in the morning, after you wake up, minutes before you go to bed, your lunch break at work, or whenever it works for you.
- Decide how much time you'll dedicate to the task at hand. I almost never spend more than thirty minutes a day.
- Don't break the chain! There are no days off, not even the weekend. If that sounds too hard for you, lower the time to twenty or fifteen minutes, but you have to do it every day. No excuses (However, if you have absolutely no choice but to skip a day or two, all isn't lost. Just make sure you start over the next day).

Are you thinking, "But, but … how do I get myself to start studying?"

Here's a small trick you can use to convince yourself to start doing a task. Tell yourself, "I'll only do this for five minutes. Then I'll stop."

Five minutes is next to nothing, so it shouldn't be that hard to get started. You're highly likely to spend more than five minutes studying the language, but the toughest part is getting started, and this trick facilitates it for you.

Are you now thinking, "But, but … I don't have time to do that! I'm too busy!"?

Does that mean you don't have thirty minutes in twenty-four hours? Are you sure? What about the time you spend monitoring your social media, watching TV, or mindlessly surfing the Internet? What about the time you spend waiting for something? Would waking up thirty minutes earlier or going to bed thirty minutes later make much of a difference? If you don't have time, make time.

Is this question now running through your mind: "But, but ... can I really learn anything in just thirty minutes?"

Don't expect the first day to work wonders for you. The key is repetition. Try doing this for a week. After that, how about a month? The results will surprise you: I guarantee. If you want to achieve your goals, you'll have to do something to work toward them every day. No matter how insignificant one day's study session might seem to you, it's very important in the long run, and it's the simplest, most effective way to bring yourself closer to what you want to achieve.

Do you want to learn a language? Yes? Then what can you do about it today?

You can choose to learn your new language every day. Wake up and say, "I'll learn Japanese" If it helps, spice it up a bit: "I'll learn some Japanese today. I'll master how to say XXX in Japanese today" where XXX is anything in the world you'd like to obtain how to say in your new language, in this case Japanese. That way you'll have a choice and a sense of purpose valid for today only.

Try not to set a goal you know you can't achieve, though. For example, learning fifty new words a day is a bit too much, so make sure you set an objective you know you can achieve. Be realistic and go for it; program your mind.

Always move at your own pace. If, for example, your initial plan was to learn five phrases today but you didn't make it, learn four phrases instead. If you want to learn how to pronounce a long word but you can't do it today, break the word into chunks and learn to pronounce the first one today, the next one tomorrow, and so on, until you can pronounce the whole word (this is how I learned to pronounce long German words as a beginner). Break any task you can't manage into small chunks you can manage. This will help you learn the entire task and experience the joy of completing a chunk every day.

Don't try to learn the language "in six months." Rather, learn exactly what you want in the language and choose to learn your language today. And the day after that. And the day after that. With this method, "Learn Hindi in six months" becomes "Learn how to say XXX in Hindi today."

See the difference?

Trust me—all these "todays" can add up to something magical.

Learn to take action. If you don't act, you don't get. Learn to adapt to change. You need to change what you've been doing up to now so that you can have different results from what you've had up to now. Learn to learn. Language learning can be time-consuming, and you won't see big results immediately. If you're smart and you cut the process into small, manageable chunks that bring instant results, then you're halfway through.

Learning a language is like riding a bike. Once you learn how to do it, you can do it again and again and again.

SAMPLE ROUTINE YOU CAN USE

Here's a sample routine you can use to learn a language:

Follow a method or two intended for language learning. These will be your main methods. (Examples of main methods include Duolingo, YouTube videos for language learning, language-specific online courses, and any other free online language course.)

Supplement the main methods with media and other fun activities that can help you learn a language. (Examples of other activities include movies and radio for listening, Memrise for vocabulary, and Italki discussions for grammar and writing.)

My routine changes from language to language, but the core philosophy of it is:

- Collecting phrases (not words)
- Filtering these phrases by personal preference at the moment: What do I want to learn right now? What expresses my feelings or what I want to talk about right now?
- Checking the filtered phrases: Are they grammatically correct? Do native speakers use them? Which part of the phrase do I know already? What words are unfamiliar to me? How is it pronounced?
- Studying and repeating the phrases so that they get in my head

- Using the phrases (by talking either to myself or with other people, entering them into whatever conversation I'm having)
- Repeating the whole process

I also supplement this with a dedicated free language course or platform, if I can find any in the language I want to learn. I keep using this dedicated site or platform until I reach a conversational level in the language, then I only use my own routine together with more videos, movies, news sites or blogs, or anything else I want to read at any time of day.

Whenever I'm unsure about what to learn in my new language, I think of my native language. *Don't I use certain phrases (or small sets of words) more than others? Aren't there things I use every day? Don't I learn new words in my native language and gradually incorporate them into my everyday life? Don't I sometimes make spelling or grammatical mistakes in my own language? Why do I tolerate this in my own language, yet I can't do the same for my new one, which I happen to be learning anyway? Am I not being too hard on myself? Isn't that unfair?*

The following illustrates my routine in detail (I almost always learn new vocabulary and grammar by necessity).

STEP 1: THE SOURCE

Select sources for words and phrases in your target language. This could be Duolingo, Memrise, Readlang, YouTube, a blog post, an article, a video game, a native speaker, or any other source you prefer.

STEP 2: STUDYING THE WORD/PHRASE

The way that you study the words and phrases you've found varies by source: you may just study them through Duolingo or Memrise, you may store them in flashcards or any SRS software, you may write them down somewhere, or you may just save them somewhere for a quick review.

Most language learners' studying routines finish here, after Step 2. But is that all you can do? Have you reached your full potential?

No!

The following are some other stages that most language learners don't follow.

STEP 3: RESEARCH ON GOOGLE TO SEE HOW NATIVE SPEAKERS USE THE WORD/PHRASE

Most language learners forget one crucial thing about languages: they're forms of communication! While an academic approach to a language isn't bad, especially if you want to delve deep into reading/writing books and essays, sometimes it's important to remember that people speak these languages! So how do native speakers use these phrases?

If you don't have the luxury of living in a country where people speak your target language, use Google to look up how people use the words you've just learned. What a find, eh? We've already talked about that, and yet most people don't do this. Believe me, though, it helps a lot, especially in the beginning stages.

STEP 4: FIND AND TRANSLATE ALTERNATIVE PHRASES

Google doesn't understand that you're learning the language, so it will show you phrases that probably don't correspond to what you'd like to learn in the early stages, or phrases you don't understand. When that happens, the fast solution to the problem is to use another, rather famous Google tool: Google translate.

Find and copy any phrase that seems interesting to you, and plug it into Google Translate. If it looks like something you'd most likely use in the initial stages, just take it as it comes and store it in flash cards or your favorite learning method.

Next, you should use the "let's make sure we're correct" solution: Use Google Translate again, but then paste that phrase in HiNative and ask native speakers to tell you what it means and if they'd use it. Here's where the fun begins!

After you've got a list of some cool phrases, try to personalize them to match what you want to say by changing the verbs, the nouns, or any other word you want. Then write a nice little paragraph about yourself (or anything else that interests you), and send it to natives to correct using HiNative.

After you get corrected, you may notice that in some corrected phrases, words or letters change in unfamiliar ways. You don't understand why this happens, but these phrases are so nice and interesting and you want to use them! Where do these changes to the words come from, and what can you do to learn to apply them to create more phrases?

This is where grammar helps! That's when you'll want to use any of the methods under the "Grammar" chapter to find out what's happening.

STEP 5: LEARN THE NEW PHRASES

Make sure you add these new, corrected phrases to your favorite SRS or your notepad.

STEP 6: USE THE NEW PHRASES

As soon as you learn the phrases and the grammar behind them, it's time to use them in practice! You can talk to yourself using them, text a native speaker, schedule a conversation, write a diary entry, look them up on YouTube to see if you can find a relevant video, or visit a language cafe. All that matters is that you're using the phrases so that you become more confident and cement the new memories.

That's more or less the routine I follow after I've learned the basics in a language. I also use media during my dead time, like radio, music in the target language, a movie on Netflix, or an e-book in the target language.

Your routine may be very different from this, as you may learn differently, have other goals in the language, and prefer other methods. That's perfectly fine. There isn't one way of learning languages.

MOTIVATION

We often hear this word when people talk about learning languages or any other skill, for that matter.

"I tried to learn Japanese, but lost motivation and gave it up a few weeks later."

"I know I have to learn Chinese at some point, but I just have no motivation to do it."

Most people believe that without motivation, you can't learn a language, and they're partially right. Motivation is imperative, so that you can keep going. But how can you get motivated? It's simpler than you think.

Taking action is all you have to do to get motivated. Start with the language. Dive deeper. That's where you'll find the motivation you're seeking. You don't need motivation to take action; you need to take action to gain motivation.

If you do this and follow the process we discussed of breaking big tasks into smaller, manageable daily chunks, you'll start to feel motivated. You'll become more interested in the language because you'll be happy you took action. By following this process, you'll gain so much more than just motivation.

Let's look at an example of a small call to action that can lead to great results. A powerful tool to boost your motivation and confidence is to act, dream, and visualize.

As you already know, I enjoy talking to myself while learning a language. I've created a mini ritual that's a big help when it comes to me getting that "natural-sounding" flow some people praise.

Whenever I learn a new word, I try to create a phrase in my head into which I can insert this word. Once I've come up with a new phrase, I try to act with myself and say it out loud. For that, I really enjoy pretending to talk to someone else and entering this phrase in the conversation, just as if I'd said it a million times before (which is basically what native speakers do in their language). So at that moment, I'm acting as if I were a native speaker, too.

What do I gain? I repeat some phrases over and over again while acting, and that boosts my confidence and my speaking speed. I also get used to the new sounds and make less and less of an effort to reproduce them. So without even knowing it, I also improve my accent!

And in the middle of my fake conversation with a nonexistent person, this time without a phone, I sometimes stop to think*, Hey wait. Was that me who spoke that language at that speed? How can this be possible? I'm awesome!* Yes, I sometimes have a momentary lapse of self-appreciation and extreme satisfaction.

See how far a small step can take you?

This is one of the reasons I firmly believe effective language learning is all about psychology. It's about studying and discipline too, but psychology does play an important part, as we'll see in Section 4.

SMALL VICTORIES IN LANGUAGE LEARNING

One of the biggest mistakes you can make when learning a language is to compare your learning style or learning speed to that of others. Your language learning journey is personal. Even if you hold yourself accountable to someone else, be it a fellow learner, a parent, or a friend, how fast you advance during your journey has to do with you and you alone. If you're learning with someone else and you use the same language learning materials, you might learn at different speeds.

This is nothing to be ashamed of, honestly. I'm extremely slow at accumulating certain language learning traits and faster at others. I'm slow at learning and remembering new vocabulary, but I can pick up the accent of a language fast. Each person is different, and that's okay. As mentioned previously in this book, you want to make use of your personal learning characteristics and turn your weaknesses into strengths.

That's where celebrating your small victories comes into play.

If, for example, you understand somebody speaking your target language for the first time (even if that person says just one sentence), that's something to celebrate—especially if you previously had a hard time understanding anything in the language. It's not the time to think about what others are doing.

It's very easy to fall into the trap of saying, "Oh, well. I understood a sentence. Others can understand a person much easier. I'm not as good as them. I'm bad at languages. Maybe I should give up?" And it's a downward spiral from there. You know how your mind works, going from bad thought to worse until it completely sabotages you and you end up giving up.

Instead, why don't you try this: "Until yesterday, I couldn't understand anything people were saying in my target language. I perceived just weird sounds, and I had to take time to think about them so that my brain would convert them into words I could understand. That took too much time, and I completely lost it. But today, this didn't happen! I understood what a native speaker said! I'm getting better!"

Do you notice the difference? That's how it is! You're getting better.

It doesn't matter what others achieve. If you're better than before, no matter how much better, this is something to celebrate. It feels like passing an exam and knowing that all your studying was worth it, that all your efforts paid off. Despite your concerns about not doing enough, you still achieved something, you reached a goal, and that's a clear indicator that you're on the right path.

If you stop to recognize and reward yourself for your improvement, not only will you feel great, but you'll also gain extra motivation and the boost you need to keep going. It's a win-win!-

There are other small victories to consider celebrating:

- Completing a small chunk of a task, as we previously discussed
- Getting the gist of a text, however small, for the first time
- Understanding a joke in your target language
- Telling a joke in your target language (not by translating a joke you already know—rather, using humor anew in the foreign language)

What I'd like you to do now is set aside ten minutes to write about how you'll reward yourself every time you experience one of these small victories.

Your rewards can be anything in the world, such as:

- Watching TV or spending time doing anything that pleases you after completing your study session
- Taking a walk in the park
- Going to the movies
- Eating out alone
- Buying yourself a nice bottle of wine

Your reward can be anything, as long as you recognize your achievement, pat yourself on the back, and then move on.

The healthiest comparison is comparing yourself to how you were before. It's not comparing yourself to others. Even if you believe your achievement might seem obvious to other learners, it's not obvious to you, and that's what matters.

I've caught myself saying (way too many times), "What's going on, Maria? You've been learning that language for so long and you don't even know that? That's basic knowledge!" I've said this more times than I can count, and certainly more times than I want to hear it.

Although I still say that from time to time, I've learned not to let this bring me down, and to do something about it instead. I also recognize that hey! I probably didn't learn this because I hadn't needed to use it yet, but it's never too late. Now that I came across it, I'll definitely collect it, put it in an SRS or write it down in my notebook, and learn it. As soon as I learn it, I'll reward myself.

No matter how basic you think something is in your target language, if you've never used it, you probably don't know it. And that's perfectly fine.

It's never too late to learn something new in the language. Do you know how many times I learned something in my native language way later than anyone else? I'm not even talking about my childhood years; I'm talking about now—even as we speak. There's nothing wrong with that! This happens in language learning. It doesn't mean you're not good enough, and it's certainly nothing to be embarrassed about ever.

Sometimes we're too hard on ourselves, comparing ourselves to The Ideal Learner (as I like to call that perfect learner we have in our heads and to whom we compare ourselves). The problem is, The Ideal Learner doesn't exist!

Even all those polyglots you may see speaking a foreign language fluently without hesitation have these moments from time to time. They make numerous mistakes, they may have learned some basic insights about that language recently, and they may have used something in that video you saw that they learned the previous day—or even minutes before speaking in that language! So what?

As long as you keep learning and have an open mind about everything you don't know, you'll be fine. If you don't yet know something you consider basic in the language, or something that "you should have known but don't," please just learn it and move on.

Remember, as language learners we use everything to our advantage. We don't let anything bring us down. That's how we become better and eventually fluent.

Even if you make the same mistake again and again. Even if you still can't remember a certain word. It doesn't matter. Try to learn it again. You'll get used to it!

At this point, you might nod along and think that all this sounds very good in theory. But what about in practice?

Let's face it: there will be times when you'll feel like you're not learning anything new anymore. There will be things you won't be able to understand and things you won't be able to talk about right away. There will be a certain word order, a weird secondary sentence, something that makes little to no sense in your native language (or in any other language you might know), and you won't understand it—for days, even months of everyday learning.

You'll probably have some clumsy conversations, even if your language is at a very decent level. At times you won't feel like studying your target language. Life will get in the way. You'll doubt yourself. You'll even wonder, what's the point of trying anyway? …

This is perfectly normal. It happens to me from time to time, even after having learned many languages. It happens to all of us, no exceptions.

This is because the process of learning a language isn't linear. It's a journey with ups but also quite a few downs. In the next chapter, I'll try to cover as many downs as possible and show you what you can do to stay focused and motivated despite experiencing them.

SECTION 4

Troubleshooting

"Keep going, because you did not come this far just to come this far."

—Anonymous

LANGUAGE LEARNING FAILURES

Language learning can be a long journey, and as any journey that has to do with learning new skills, it has its ups and downs.

What distinguishes polyglots or successful language learners from other people is, first, they know how to handle failure and choose to keep going. Yes, all those polyglots and professionals that use many languages on a daily basis have had failures. Big ones. And a lot of embarrassment—just like you and me. I've also had quite a few failures learning and using all my languages. I'd like to share some with you and let you know what I did to overcome them.

You see, you're not special for failing at even the most basic components of a language. It's not that you're an idiot and all others have it a lot easier. It happens to everyone. Let's see how I failed.

As I previously discussed in the chapter about talking to yourself under Section 2, I've put up a video of me speaking in Basque online. That video went viral in the Basque Country, so Basque TV and radio stations approached me for an interview. Learning Basque as a foreigner who has nothing to do with the Basque Country whatsoever is unusual. So a local radio station in Basque invited me for an interview at their headquarters.

On the day of the interview, when I arrived at the headquarters' building, I met a woman there. I didn't even have to tell her who I was because she recognized me; we had a small chitchat in Basque, and she directed me to the room where I'd have a live interview with another woman there.

Everything was going great. We talked a bit with the woman who would interview me. She gave me some instructions and then turned on the mic. As soon as she did that and asked me the first question, I went silent. Nothing was coming out of my mouth. I understood the question she asked me—it was simple and had to do with what I'd done in Bilbao the previous day—but still, no words would come out of my mouth.

I was totally stressed out and didn't know what to do. I instantly thought, *Oh boy, what's going on? Suddenly I can't speak a word of Basque! People will think I'm a fraud and my video was fake! People will think I scripted everything and I know nothing in Basque! That's it,"* I resolved. *"I'm done with Basque and languages in general. That's too much to handle.* All these thoughts went through my mind at lightning speed, making me even more unable to utter a word.

The woman started to look a bit disturbed, yet she didn't react badly. She seemed like she understood what was going on and turned off the mic. We agreed we'd try again, but I asked her to turn it off again even before she could ask me the first question. It was a complete failure. She told me we'd postpone that interview for another day, and I shouldn't worry too much.

In my head, it was a complete failure. She was trying to be kind to me, but she also thought I was a fraud and I couldn't speak the language. Shame, stress, cold sweat, and the imposter syndrome at its finest!

We went outside the building and got into her car. She took me to the nearest bus station where I'd take the bus back to Vitoria, the city where I was staying. I was still so stressed I spoke a mix of Basque and Spanish to her. As soon as she left me at the station and drove away, I covered my face in my hands. *How was that possible?! Why on earth did that happen? Why am I so bad at Basque?*

I didn't want to speak that language again that day. Even though before I went to the radio headquarters, I'd spoken Basque to everyone on the street, asking them for directions or to take photos of me, that was over. No more Basque! I was terrible at it, I thought.

A few hours later, as I was strolling on the street in the same city, waiting for my bus to come and trying to enjoy the beauty of the city without thinking of my linguistic incompetence, a young man approached me. He said he wasn't from the city and needed instructions to get to a certain monument. He spoke in Basque to me because I was carrying a newspaper in Basque. As I'd also visited that monument a few moments prior, I gave him instructions—in Basque—to get there.

This time, I'd no difficulty whatsoever telling him where to go and what to do, so I spoke Basque again, and this time it worked. He thanked me and left. Right after that, I felt like something was changing in the wind. *Hey, my Basque isn't that terrible, after all!* I thought. *Maybe something else was wrong? Perhaps I'm too nervous in front of a camera or a microphone, and I also felt I somehow had to prove to the world how well I speak Basque, and that was a killer combination that damaged me?*

I even pictured the woman trying to interview me a few hours earlier. I mentally replayed the question she asked me and tried to answer it in my head in Basque. This time everything worked. I could answer that question in Basque! "So," I thought, "okay, I'll keep learning that language. That wasn't as bad as I thought, after all."

Back then, I wasn't that experienced with language learning, so after that failed interview, I was sure I'd quit Basque. Had that young man never approached me, I would never have tried learning Basque (or any other language) ever again.

This experience made me think, *What if every time I fail in a language, I keep going? What if every time I fail in a language, it's actually an indicator of what I have to improve, not how incompetent I am at languages and that I have to give up language learning?*

As soon as I started asking myself these questions, everything cleared up for me. I would never quit a language after a failure because the reasons I wanted to become fluent in the first place were a lot stronger than what happened to me. Also, what happened to me was meant to happen, so that I could realize what I needed to improve.

With Basque, I had to overcome that huge difficulty of talking to natives, which would take me years to accomplish. I actually just achieved this goal this year, even though the incident in Basque happened in 2014, but I knew that was the kick in the butt I needed to start the recovery procedure.

Another failure had to do with my efforts to learn Hungarian. I moved to Budapest for some time, since I had an online job and I could move anywhere I wanted, and I had difficulties understanding Hungarians most times. I used the wrong words. I said embarrassing things to people that mattered, and I also said something insulting to someone I had a crush on.

I was trying to be sarcastic in Hungarian, but sadly, it didn't work. That person was hugely offended, even after my cries that it wasn't my mother tongue, I didn't mean to say it like that, and it was just sarcasm. I was devastated. I couldn't sleep all night, and I cursed myself for even taking up Hungarian. I doubted my language learning skills again.

But I also remembered the incident in Basque, so this failure showed that that type of sarcasm doesn't work in Hungarian. It also taught me that there's a lot more to a language than just grammar, vocabulary, and sounds—there's a whole culture behind it. I needed to work on my vocabulary, so that I could find synonyms for some words I used that carry a strong, often insulting meaning.

That experience was another indicator. I had to work on my vocabulary and watch my mouth and my humor in Hungary. I kept going with my efforts to learn Hungarian, and the rewards I received outweighed the failures by far. People invited me to houses where amazing Hungarian families lived and prepared some very tasty food for me (As soon as you visit their homes, Hungarians love to stuff you with food until you're full, and then stuff you even more. They're amazing). I also made some great friends and spoke my way out of very difficult situations where English wouldn't have worked. I'm happy I kept going!

These are just two of my epic failures in all my languages, but I choose to do as polyglots do: I seek to understand what's behind every failure and work on it, I try to take something positive out of each failure, and I keep going. That's why I succeed.

Everything deserves another chance. When you're about to quit, try one more time.

It's easy to get frustrated and quit. Putting an immediate end to whatever you've been striving to learn, no matter how long you've been at it, is simple. I can't tell you how many times I've quit learning a language. I'd given up on German three times before I finally learned it. Every one of those times I failed, I was absolutely frustrated or bored, and I decided to put an end to German learning on a whim. Just like that.

Even the last time I took up German and became committed to it, I was seriously thinking about quitting. I was experienced; after all, I'd already done it three times. What would a fourth time be? Nothing important, easy-peasy, lemon squeezy. I'm out. And then I asked myself the question that made me reconsider: *What if I tried one more time?*

Maybe there's something I haven't tried yet, I thought. *Perhaps I'll make it work this time? I'll possibly regret my decision to quit, just like I did the three other times I quit. So why not give it one more try? Just one. Then I'll ditch it for good.*

That was it! I made a promise to myself that I would ask that question every single time I was about to quit. And here I am, living in Germany, speaking no other language than German to do everything here. I'm so glad I didn't quit. The joys the German language has given me outweigh all embarrassment and frustrations by far.

So before you quit a language for good, ask yourself, "What if I tried one more time?"

My failures also taught me to take language learning seriously, but not to take myself seriously. What does that mean? Let's find out.

Has one of these situations ever happened to you?

Scenario 1: You've finally booked a conversation with a native speaker on Skype. Minutes before your call, your palms are sweaty, and you desperately look up phrases and answers you've compiled to questions the person might ask you. You feel scheduling this call wasn't a wise decision. You're not ready yet! You should have waited longer before doing this. What were you thinking?

Then the call starts with introductory phrases. Of course you know these. You'll nail them. You're starting to speak fast when suddenly … you get corrected. There was a mistake there! You completely lose yourself and panic. You're guilty. Words won't come out of your mouth anymore. You want out! How could you make such a mistake? You knew these phrases already, didn't you? You were supposed to make mistakes later, not while talking about yourself! You knew these things!

Scenario 2: At last, it's time to speak with a native speaker! It's your time to shine and show them how well you speak! You've talked to yourself while cleaning, listened to podcasts while driving, and watched your favorite series, and you can construct lots of phrases in your head. You say some out loud to yourself. "If he asks me where I work, I'll tell him about my work and I'll even add what my dream job would be." You keep talking to yourself in your target language fast and without hesitation. You're pumped up. Ready? Set? Go!

The call starts. As soon as you hear the native speaker's first phrases, you freeze completely. You're not able to utter a word. What's going on? You're so good—what happened? You lose control. You hate yourself. You pretend the line's not working properly, and you sign out, feeling completely betrayed by yourself. How could this happen to you?

Do you notice what these two scenarios have in common?

You're taking yourself too seriously.

What are you trying to prove? Why have such high expectations? Why would you be taken away by just one mistake? Why were you supposed to perform perfectly? Who do you think you are?

Did you notice anything else?

The only one responsible for your panic was you. Your language buddy didn't think anything you thought they did. You were just imagining what they might have thought and sabotaging yourself for no reason.

Your language buddy corrected you so that you could learn from your mistakes and become better. He didn't think you'd pillaged his language. Most native speakers are glad you're even trying to learn their language!

If this sounds like you, fear not. I used to be such a perfectionist, and the two scenarios I described above have happened to me. I almost started hitting myself afterwards.

But now, as I'm trying to overcome perfectionism, I find there are a lot of things that don't make sense. What if I made no mistakes at all? What if I nailed every single phrase in the target language?

It happened to me once, which made me happy, but soon enough I realized something: speaking perfectly the first time you try is probably the worst thing that can happen to you.

While it's highly pleasant, it can make you set such high expectations of yourself that you get anxious and drown in your own thoughts. You forget why you even started this language journey. Wasn't it because you were interested in the language? Wasn't it because you wanted to communicate? To have fun?

If you magically say everything correctly, you try to force yourself to live up to your own expectations that you'll always speak that way. That's anything but pleasant. It's torture! I've been there; I've done that. In retrospect, I wish I'd made a mistake or two because that makes me feel like I'm finally allowed to relax and stop trying to satisfy the needs I thought my language buddy had.

But what if you're just too afraid of making mistakes?

DOUBTING YOURSELF

There will be moments you'll doubt your language skills. You'll question yourself: "Why am I doing this? … I'm not ready to do X thing. … I'm so afraid of making mistakes. … Maybe language learning isn't for me—who am I trying to kid anyway?"

I have something to confess to you.

I've been teaching myself languages for seven years now, and I've learned many languages and improved many aspects about myself along the way. But something has always been constant.

Doubt.

Even if days have passed, and it doesn't seem to be there anymore, doubt somehow finds a way to come back from time to time. I still doubt my language skills in each and every one of my languages—not all the time, but it still happens.

For example, at times I doubt my ability to communicate effectively in German at work, or even right before making a phone call. Even though I've done this many times, if I'm going to be talking about a topic I'm not familiar with yet or I haven't talked about before, I feel uneasy.

Will I be able to say exactly what I want? Can people understand me? Will I understand everything said to me from the other side of the phone?

Or when I want to talk to another person about anything at all, sometimes I stop to think whether what I said was right or made any sense, right after having spoken in my target language, no matter how well I speak it. Even in my strongest languages (and sometimes even in my native language), I still have doubts.

So if you have doubts and are questioning your language learning abilities, please don't worry. This is a perfectly normal part of language learning, and it's actually a good thing; you can take advantage of it. Instead of wondering, "How could this happen to me? I've been studying that language for X amount of time and I still sometimes feel uneasy. Am I that horrible? Are my skills that bad?"

You could replace this self-sabotaging talk with questions like: "How can I use this to my advantage? How does this help me become better?"

Then, suddenly, a world of opportunity pops in. Having doubts about your language skills makes you become better in the language. Questioning what you want to say during a phone call or a conversation with a native speaker makes you research whether what you want to say is right. Doing this research also introduces more things you could talk about, or even possibilities of what the other person might say, making you better in the language in the process!

Your worries and doubts make you create new language learning material! Then what you do is write down that new material, possibly using it with a native speaker afterward. So by having those doubts, you've collected, learned, and used new learning material!

You should pat yourself on the back for those uncomfortable feelings. They're your friends!

Succeeding in language learning means turning your weaknesses into strengths. This is a powerful tool you can learn to use that'll come in handy in other skills and areas in your life.

I learned how to use this tool through language learning, and it's made me better at all life's challenges as well as other skills I wanted to learn. This made me finally get around to writing the book you're reading right now.

Sometimes our own worst enemies are ourselves. In language learning, our own worst (and only) enemy is always ourselves.

Even if a person comes up to you and mocks your language skills, laughs at your accent, tells you you'll never learn your target language, or encourages you to give up, your worst enemy is still yourself. Not that person. Most of the time, these people have never tried to learn a foreign language, so they don't know how hard it can be. They don't understand that exposing your language skills to others, no matter at what level you are, is a sign of bravery. You're very brave for doing this.

These people might also be jealous. They might have tried to learn a foreign language but gave up or failed. They stopped while you kept going; they recognize this and feel bad about themselves, so they want to make you feel miserable so that they can feel better.

In any case, you're your own enemy, and if you let their comments affect you, your enemy's won. You've lost the game and stopped learning your target language.

My advice to myself is always this: "Keep going and be patient." These simple, strong words make it all possible.

MAKING MISTAKES

Do you make mistakes often when you speak in your target language? Do you feel frustrated whenever people correct you? Does it make you want to stop learning the language because you feel you'll never be able to learn it?

If your answer is yes and you nodded along, then congratulations. There's nothing wrong with you.

Making errors feels so bad to us because we've been taught that way. It's highly likely you have some memory of a teacher or a parent yelling (at you or someone else), "It's like that! Not like that! That's wrong!" as if it were the end of the world, embarrassing you or that other child.

I could simply tell you right here that you should overcome that fear. You shouldn't be afraid of making flaws, right?

Right. You understand that. Yet you're still afraid.

Until recently, I was also terrified of making mistakes. Yes, even well into my language learning journey, after success stories with Spanish and Basque, I was afraid of making mistakes. I still am from time to time. This is normal, and it's something else you can use to your advantage.

Hey, being afraid of making mistakes is just another form of sabotaging yourself, so my previous advice still applies: "How can I use this to become better? How can I use it to my advantage?"

If you're afraid of making mistakes, as soon as you make them and get corrected, you feel bad, but it's very unlikely that you'll forget these errors. This means you'll remember the correct versions!

The bad thing about being afraid of making mistakes, though, is that you might not give yourself that many opportunities to speak your target language. What will really happen, though, if you make mistakes? What will a native speaker really think of you? What's the worst thing that could happen?

Do you think the earth will split into two pieces right at the spot where you're standing because you conjugated that verb wrong? Do you think the native speaker that's listening to you will suddenly turn into a monster (or worse, your strict schoolteacher from third grade), grab a huge ruler, and start hitting you, shouting the correct version of the verb you should have said?

Will the world ban you from speaking your target language for life for breaching its masterfully crafted verb-conjugation rules? Will the language banning committee send you threatening messages?

Of course not! None of these things will happen!

I'll tell you another secret: your worst fears and worries of what might happen never happen.

Think of any worry and fear you had about anything in your life. Did it actually occur exactly as you pictured it in your mind? I highly doubt it.

Granted, at times, terrible things happen. But in 99 percent of the situations, your worst fears do not happen, not in the way you pictured.

So please relax. Free yourself. Make those mistakes and correct them. They're your best friends, and, like all best friends, they want to be by your side from time to time. Let them be. And, like your best friends, show them that you care about them and correct them!

It's no big deal, really. I've made so many mistakes, I've been embarrassed so many times, words can't describe how bad I've felt for making mistakes in my foreign languages. I try to imagine what the people who heard me are thinking: "She made that stupid mistake! And how long has she been learning that language? Two years? Seriously? She's a joke!" I usually think that all people that hear my mistakes think things like that—or even worse.

You know what all these people are actually thinking? I'll tell you another secret: They're thinking about themselves. Even when you've made a mistake and they corrected you, the most probable thing they'll think is this: "Was I too rude when I pointed out her mistake and corrected her? Will she talk to me again? Was I speaking clearly so she could understand what I said?"

Do you see? It's all about them, not about you. What you're doing, they're doing for themselves too. You're thinking that perhaps you weren't good enough, and that's what they're thinking about themselves, too.

That's how we work as humans. That's how we live and survive. That's how we roll. We're so busy thinking of ourselves and what we did, right or wrong, that we forget others do the same.

So there's no reason that we should worry that much. We're not the center of the universe, fortunately! We're not as important to others as we think we are, and that's liberating!

My advice is the next time you make mistakes and you realize it, just try to correct them and move on. Next time you won't make the same mistakes, although you might make new ones—and that's a good thing.

I've met polyglots and language learners that set a personal goal to make as many mistakes as possible. That's how they improve. There are even people that beg native speakers to correct them—they'll even buy them a beer every time they make a mistake (which breaches our "fluent for free" rule, so I don't officially recommend it, especially in certain countries where alcohol is very expensive).

Mistakes are a good thing. I know it sounds counterintuitive, but they really are our best teachers, our best friends.

As a kid, you were introduced to your language by listening to it. At one point you started speaking it, and naturally, you made mistakes and people corrected you. Those people would correct you and help you speak right, never stopping to think anything other than: "This is totally normal. They're just a kid, and they'll learn with time."

The same thing happens when you're learning a new language.

People will react to your mistakes differently, since you're an adult now, but the core message won't change at all. They'll probably think, "This is totally normal. They're a foreigner trying to learn my language. They're a beginner, and my language is hard. They'll learn with time."

What's the best thing about this? They won't even think about that! It's perfectly normal!

Are you wondering what native speakers really think?

They're impressed by the mere fact that you're learning their language! The rarer the language, the more excited they'll get. They'll either do their best to facilitate your learning the language (which is a plus), or they might tell you, "Don't worry, our language is really hard to learn" (which is also a plus, because it's a challenge!). They also may not correct you, so that you won't feel bad about yourself.

The third option is the one you most probably prefer, especially while chatting to them, but believe me, this one is the worst. You won't get corrected, so you won't recognize your mistakes, which means you won't make any progress in your language. Feeling a bit better at that moment will sacrifice your own improvement! It's like putting off that special project you need to keep doing because you prefer to message your friends on Facebook or spend a few hours watching cat videos on YouTube.

You'll be happy in the short run but frustrated in the long run because you won't have made any progress, and you'll tell yourself all the wrong reasons why you haven't: "Languages aren't for me. ... I'll never learn it. ... What was I thinking? ... I don't have the language gene." Do these ring a bell?

But what if the native speakers really tell me off?

That almost never happens (in my case, I've yet to come across such people and I'm learning my ninth language now, mind you!), but even if it does, I've got something for you. In all aspects of your life, don't you want to be surrounded by the right people? Be it your family, your friends, some co-workers you've handpicked? Why wouldn't you do that in language learning?

Choose people that are learning your language, or any other language, so that they can understand what you're experiencing. There are a lot of language exchange sites out there, and a handful of "5 black cats" shouldn't prevent you from looking.

Let's talk about the benefits of learning to accept that you'll make mistakes.

At this point, you probably know that I believe language learning is all about psychology. Apart from languages, it teaches you life skills. By learning to accept the fact that you'll make mistakes, being open to that, learning from the mistakes, and stopping yourself from taking yourself too seriously, you'll also change as a person. Accepting your mistakes and trying to correct them is a simple skill that can unlock all your potential in all fields of your life.

I've a small challenge for you. The next time you schedule a conversation with a native speaker, in addition to the time you spend prior to the conversation preparing some phrases and scripts, set aside five to ten minutes and simply talk to yourself. Ask the following questions:

- What will happen if I make mistakes and get corrected?
- What if I don't take myself too seriously this time?
- Why shouldn't I have some fun instead of being terrorized by my own thoughts?
- What do I have to lose?
- What do I have to gain?

Try to answer these questions, then try to evaluate how important your reasons are. I can tell you right now, they're not important. It's just your brain spewing evil words at you.

Feel the fear, and do it anyway. The magic always happens outside your comfort zone. You'll be happy you did it.

Apart from the psychological factor, what more can you gain from this? A paper or a notepad full of corrected mistakes—and that's when you have to take yourself seriously again. You need to make sure to study it and try not to make the same mistakes again.

Even if you do make the same mistakes, though, no worries! Repetition is the key to success. You'll get corrected again, this will ring a bell for you, and it'll be even easier to correct it.

Go make mistakes now and have some fun!

"I CAN'T GET BETTER!" - LEARNING PLATEAU

You've started your language journey. Having found your favorite methods and created your learning routine, you're learning consistently and feeling confident about it. For some time now you've seen improvement in your language skills, and it looks like it's only getting better.

After a while, though, those exciting linguistic gains you had start to slow. You might complain about how slowly you're learning now compared to the beginning, and it's taking a toll on your motivation. As time passes, these gains almost disappear. No matter what you do, everything feels like a chore because you're not really improving anymore. That's when you know you've hit a learning plateau—a place where you don't seem to get better in the language anymore and your motivation decreases significantly.

That's when many people stop learning a language. It's a common problem, not only in language learning, but with any other skills you want to improve. At first, we learn quickly until we reach the intermediate level, where learning slows down a bit. It's normal to want to give up at this point. We know enough already, don't we? Most people stop getting better at this point and remain in limbo.

But greatness and, in our case, fluency are on the other side of that plateau. Your bigger language learning goals are probably on that other side too. It's critical to break yourself out of that plateau so that you keep learning and getting better.

Are you wondering how can you do that?

First, you need to identify what's stopping you. Is there anything in particular that prevents you from taking that step and becoming better? Is it a method you got tired of, or is it something deeper?

Most of the time, what happens is that, after improving your language skills, you hit a point where a particular challenge makes that learning plateau comfortable for you. For example, the plateau helps you avoid something you find scary.

If you've been talking to yourself but you're too embarrassed to speak to other people and have been avoiding it, there's your answer. If you've been listening to podcasts about how to learn your target language but still haven't watched your favorite movie without subtitles (fearing you won't understand what's going on), that's your answer. If you've been writing diary entries for a long time but still haven't gotten around to publishing an article in your target language (even though you've always wanted to), you know you've hit a plateau.

Identify your biggest challenge and try to tackle it. That's where the exit from your learning plateau lies. You'll fail from time to time, but that's when you know you're making progress. Doing something you find scary is what ends up helping you grow.

If you choose to work on your challenges but you feel like you're still in a learning plateau, then other factors might be at play.

Is your learning process a bit too … predictable?

If you've been doing the same tasks repeatedly, it's easy to get stuck in a routine that may have started out as fun but which you've eventually grown tired of. How about spicing it up with unpredictable exercises?

You can start changing your focus and priorities throughout the week, making sure you spend at least one day exercising your speaking skills, then another day on your writing skills, and then another day on your grammar, depending on what you've been putting off the most. Try to change the content you study. If you've been studying basketball because you love the sport, how about studying something completely different today?

If all else fails, try mixing up your favorite methods and techniques. For example, if you use Anki to learn phrases, try recording these phrases and comparing them to how a native speaker says them. Schedule a conversation with a native speaker and have them say these phrases and record them. That's an example of mixing up techniques.

If there's something special going on in your life right now, try talking about it in your target language. Do you notice any gaps? Work on them! Work on saying exactly what you want in your target language, not only what you can. This is a great way to bust out of that plateau.

Keep challenging yourself, ask yourself how you can improve, try to overcome any limiting belief that's holding you back, and you'll get out of the plateau in no time. After that, achieving fluency will only be a matter of time.

"FINDING THE BEST METHODS FOR ME TAKES TOO MUCH TIME"

After reading Section 2 and seeing what's available out there, you might want to ask: Why should I do all of this? That can take too much time! Why not just pay for a course that's already done all these things for me so that all I have to do is actually learn instead of wasting time trying and failing? Wouldn't that be more effective?

Although the methods this book presents are free, time is money! So it's not free after all!

My answer to all those questions above is this: I feel you. But if all that's true, then why have so many people repeatedly paid for courses who can't speak or advance in their target language? These courses have already done most of that work for them: collecting language learning materials, suggesting a learning method ... Isn't that a waste of time *and* money?

Does it really have to do with paid and free material, or is it a mentality thing? I focus heavily on the mentality throughout my book for a reason.

Once you crack the code and change your mentality, once you succeed at becoming conversationally fluent in a language by using 100 percent free material and following the process of choosing a combination of methods like this book suggests, you can also make the most of paid materials, should you want to do that later. Just make sure to use their trial period (if they have one) to see if they fulfill the criteria. If they do, by all means go for it!

To actually have that mentality, though, you have to try learning for free first. After all, what do you enjoy the most? When your parents buy you a car, or when you've worked very hard to buy that car and you finally get it? Which one feels better?

Things feel way better when you've worked hard for them, which is why I always say language learning isn't easy and takes a long time. Nothing beats that sense of accomplishment. You did this alone! You did this for free! This is an experience you can't transfer to anyone else; but once you experience it, you'll see the difference—and we're talking a vast difference!

"IT GETS BORING!"

You might have heard this quote: "Choose a job you love and you'll never have to work a day in your life."

For languages, it'd be catchy to convert it into this: "Choose a language you love and you'll never have to study a day in your life."

This is a great, romantic idea of jobs and language learning; unfortunately, it's not always true. There might be 1 percent of people in this world that enjoy every minute of their jobs, but the truth is that even if you love your job, there are parts that bore you, aspects you don't enjoy that much. Unfortunately, the same is true of language learning.

If you love the language, you don't really study it; you have fun with it. But language learning isn't always fun and roses. It's also frustrating, it's also difficult, and it's also failing from time to time, becoming embarrassed, and wanting to give up. Sometimes it's even giving up and taking it up a few weeks, months, or even years later.

You have to work hard, and you have to want to put in that work, even when it gets boring, when you find something difficult to learn, or when you're trying to improve your accent and can't. So how do you keep going?

This is the first question I ask most polyglots and successful language learners after I meet them: "You've already failed like I have, you've already made your fair share of embarrassing mistakes in the language you learned like I have, you've already had one of those blackouts when words wouldn't come out of your mouth, you've already had a native speaker tell you that your skills aren't as good as you think they are ... so how do you keep going?"

I'm not interested in how they learned their languages because I know the answer to that. They picked up a couple methods that worked for them, had fun, and worked systematically. Every polyglot will tell you that. Some of them will also swear by their personal method, saying it's the absolute best there is and it guarantees fast language learning. We've already talked about this (Yes, polyglots can also believe in language learning myths!).

The truth is that their set of methods is the absolute best there is and it guarantees fast language learning ... for them! Those two tiny little words make a big world of difference. So no, I'm not interested in that response. I'm interested in how they keep going, no matter what kind of obstacle comes to them. I feel this is the quintessence of language learning.

So how do you keep going when it gets boring?

Remember the criteria we talked about when choosing a method. If you're bored, it's a red flag. You have to go back to that criteria and choose another method or different material. Try to do things you enjoy in the target language. If you have Netflix or any other channel where movies and series are available in many languages, watch everything in your target language. If you have any hobbies you could do in your target language, try to do that. If you listen to music or radio, make sure it's in your target language.

I'm learning Chinese now, and I've thought I should stop studying it more often than when I was learning other languages because of its complexity and the differences between it and everything else I know—the tones, the alphabet (it's not even an alphabet, it's a huge set of scary characters, one for each word!), the pronunciation, all of it!

These issues make it so easy and sweet to think about just giving up. But that's when I ask myself: What made me interested in the language in the first place? Why did I decide to learn it? And, apart from the obvious reasons (more job prospects, many people speak it, I'll definitely use it, it's useful to know), which never ever really drove me to learn any language, I found what I consider the most important reason that makes me stick with a language: I discovered things I love that aren't necessarily directly connected with the language.

In other words, when I think of the scary characters, I see that they allow me to do something I really love, which is drawing. When I envision of the super-hard tones, I picture my favorite hobby besides language learning, which is music. With this mindset, with this shift in my thinking, Chinese isn't an "extremely hard language." It's a different way for me to practice two things I love. So I keep on learning Chinese because it's music and art—and history, which I also happen to love.

I'm sure that, if you think hard enough, you can find other reasons why you started learning a language. They don't have to make sense to anyone else but you, and as long as parts of it speak to your heart, you'll stick with a language, no matter what.

Your motivation stems from your big "why," what you're trying to achieve with a language, and how and where you see yourself using that language. Think of all the situations and try to come up with specific examples. Make a list of your findings.

"I CAN DO BETTER, I SWEAR!"

Have you ever experienced one of those moments when you start speaking but can't remember even simple words you already know and you end up stuttering and mumbling? You swear you know way more things to say in your target language, but you've had a bad day, you're too tired, you suddenly lost your confidence, or you became so stressed words wouldn't come out.

If you've experienced this, perfect! It's normal.

And you're also normal if you thought you're terrible at languages because you can't even say what you already know, and you have to quit because who are you even kidding? It's not for you. Anyone who's ever learned a language and had to speak it at some point has suffered from this lack of self-confidence in one way or another.

Often people in Germany catch me off guard when I'm deep in my thoughts in my native language, almost living in another world while I'm doing something else, and suddenly a random German person appears out of nowhere and starts speaking to me in German, instantly shattering my own Greek-speaking world to pieces. As a result, I perform poorly in German and want to scream, "I can do better than that! I swear! My German is good!" Sometimes it's even worse than this, and I don't understand what they're talking about, even if I know all the words they use!

A good speaking performance depends on many factors. It's not as simple as we think. It's not that we can speak 100 percent to our capabilities at all times and under all circumstances. Heck, I've even had this problem in my native language, especially when I've been exhausted. Words wouldn't come out, or what I'd say would make no sense—in my native language.

There's no need to be hard on yourself with your new language. Think of what happens with your native language, and you'll realize it has nothing to do with your language skills. It has to do with your current state of body and mind. If you're too stressed to speak, like I was during my speaking exams in English, it's normal to perform poorly because part of your brain is fighting that stress instead of concentrating on your language skills.

Whenever such hard times come, please remember it's not always like that. It will get better. I'm sure you might have also experienced a situation in which you could speak well in your new language, even if you said just one or two phrases, and then you felt like you're superb at the language. It's the same thing.

The truth is somewhere in between.

You can't perform at a 100 percent at all times, not even professional interpreters can do that. You're no machine; you're a person. Sometimes words won't come out. Acknowledge it and move on.

"I'VE NO IDEA WHAT I'M DOING!"

When you're the leader of your journey and you've never done this before without a teacher or anyone to tell you what to learn and when, it's easy to get lost, become overwhelmed, wonder what you should do next, whether you're learning the right things, etc. You get in a train of thought that makes you want to scream, "I have no idea what I'm doing!"

I understand. But I have a question for you: do you think everyone always knows what they're doing?

Take successful language learners, for example. It's easy to look at them and assume that they knew exactly what they were doing right from the start, or that they had some sort of innate expertise that led them down their paths to fluency. But is that true? Rarely.

When I started teaching myself Spanish, I wasn't an expert language learner, and I didn't know every step I had to take. In fact, I had no idea what I was doing. That didn't matter to me though. I only wanted to have fun with Spanish!

That language journey ended up being successful, but all I did in practice was start from somewhere and make it all up as I went along. It wasn't always easy; it was a road with bumps and potholes, but I persisted because, while I knew nothing about language learning (other than the boring classes I once had), I wanted to figure out how I could learn Spanish for free and have fun.

So if you have no idea what you're doing, it doesn't matter! You're doing exactly the same thing all successful language learners do when they began their journeys!

"I'M NOT READY TO SPEAK TO PEOPLE!"

I can really relate to this problem in language learning because I also struggled a lot with it. I always waited, and waited, and waited … and increased the amount of work I put in on my skills … until I was finally ready to speak to native speakers.

Even if I had the illusion of being "somewhat ready" after a lot of time of getting input in the language, I'd think of all my gaps and flaws minutes before having that first conversation. I'd freak out, cancel the conversation, and hide in my shell, instantly dismissing any idea of talking to anyone in the language until I was 100 percent ready.

This took me years to master, and I'd only talk to myself or—under much pressure—talk to native speakers (but as rarely as possible) until I had a very simple thought that started changing many of my issues.

What if I'm not the only one?

What if other people struggled with feeling ready to put their language skills to actual use? What if there were many other desperate souls out there who knew they had to speak in the language but who were met with a wall painted in huge graffiti letters that shouted, "YOU'RE NOT READY!" back at them?

These questions started to free me. Then it escalated even more.

What if no one's ready?

At this point, everything started to make sense. This scattered puzzle started forming into something I could understand. All the pieces were put together as if an invisible force cast a spell on them. That's it!

No one's ready. It's just that some people choose to ignore that and keep going.

I became curious to see if that's true, so I talked to many, many polyglots and people using multiple languages at home or at work. Most of them confessed the same thing to me: They're never truly ready, yet they move forward. And that makes all the difference.

They just move on; and by repeatedly choosing to move on, they form a habit of completely ignoring the idea that they're not ready, to the point that they don't even ask themselves that question again.

So it was true after all! I followed it.

From then on, I moved on despite not feeling ready. I'm never ready to use my language skills out there, even after so many years of learning languages and becoming fluent or conversational. I still don't feel prepared to leave my apartment and into the German-speaking world, but I do it anyway.

In fact, I've reached a point where, whenever I have to have a conversation in the language I'm currently learning, I always ask myself (jokingly), "Maria, are you ready?" And my answer is, "No!"

Then I smile and say, "Perfect! Let's do this, anyway!"

So are you ready to learn a language? Are you eager to speak your new language to people? Are you excited to get out of your comfort zone and watch your language skills improve exponentially?

Are you ready to get your language skills out there, be it by speaking to a native speaker, by writing an essay or a message that a native speaker will see, or just by using the language in any way that will make it public?

No?

Perfect, let's do it, anyway!

WHEN ALL ELSE FAILS - HONEST SELF-QUESTIONING

Sometimes, especially when all else fails, honesty is the answer. Being honest with yourself is very important when it comes to language learning. You can achieve this by asking yourself the right questions. (This trick can help you gain the extra motivation you want or avoid giving up on your language learning journey when the going gets tough.)

Remember, you're the leader of the journey, so a good leader has to inspire, as well as analyze what's wrong. The hardest part of this process isn't asking honest questions; it's giving honest answers to these questions, even to yourself. Sometimes being 100 percent honest with yourself is very hard.

The following is a series of questions you can ask yourself to gain more clarity in times of (extreme) frustration.

- Why do I want to learn this language?
- What does it mean to me?
- Is what I'm doing working?
- How could I get better?
- Do I enjoy what I'm doing?
- What's the worst that can happen?

Why do I want to learn this language? Whenever I'm on the brink of quitting my target language, this is the first question I ask myself. I go back to my personal *why*. Why did I get into this? Why am I learning this language in the first place? Isn't my *why* stronger than the reason I want to quit?

This is where answering with your honest *why*, no matter how irrational it may seem to the logical side of your brain, makes all the difference. Basque was hard for me, so I continuously had to remind myself why I was learning it—to speak the language of a person I was in love with. I was thinking, "Well, I can't have you, but I can have an important part of you—your language. And I can even use it to impress you so that you can change your mind." Irrational? Possibly. But it always worked, and I got back on track.

What does this language mean to me? I like to say that I have a personal relationship with every one of my languages; I make them mine as soon as I become conversational in them. I had a Spanish phase—a year I was completely in love with Spanish—and to this day I like to think the Spanish language describes a part of me, a part of my character. What does it mean to you?

Is what I'm doing working? This is a tricky one because if you learn languages every day and you ask that question every day, it doesn't really help; you're being too hard on yourself. But it's different if you ask the same question after one or two months of learning and answer it honestly. If you're a perfectionist, your first answer might be, "Nothing's working. I'm not perfect. I don't sound like a native. Everything sucks."

That's where total honesty is very important. If on week one you weren't able to say two sentences in a row in Japanese and now you can have a basic conversation (albeit with some mistakes here and there), that's an important improvement. If you use Duolingo, for example, you get these moments of instant gratification and happiness as soon as you complete a lesson or your entire tree. But that doesn't mean you're also getting better in the language. If you're not getting better, then you can ask yourself the next question:

How could I get better? You can then think of ways to fine-tune the set of methods you already use, or you can try another method to see whether that would work better for you. Let's not forget our principles of adopting a method though: it should not only work, but it should also be fun, which leads us to the following question:

Do I enjoy what I'm doing? If the answer is no, ditch the method. Try something else because enjoying it will make you want to experience it again and again. If that enjoyment has worn off, it's time to choose another method!

Now I've saved the best for last: What's the worst thing that could happen? If I make another embarrassing mistake, what's in store for me? Will I immediately lose face and people will think I'm terrible in the language? Will two fiery dragons wearing T-shirts that say "WRONG GRAMMAR" take me and burn me to death? Apparently not. Whatever we worry about doesn't end up happening. At worst, a lighter version of what we thought happens.

Please also remember that whenever you think people will judge you for your mistakes, what they actually do is spend that time thinking about themselves. Did they sound too harsh when they pointed out your mistake? Should they not have corrected you because it makes them sound rude or offensive to you? Were they supposed to just stay silent and not help you get better? People spend most of their time thinking about themselves and what they did wrong, not you, and that's liberating.

If all these questions fail, keep going anyway. There will be a time when you'll thank yourself for that decision.

CONCLUSION

"Failure doesn't happen unless you allow it."
—Anonymous

When you're learning a language, always remember that whatever you're suffering from, whatever you're worried about, whatever bothers you, you're not the only one. It's not like others have it all figured out and you're the only one with serious problems. You're no worse than the others; you have the same struggles they have or that they once had. That's how life is.

So if you have any struggles with language learning, try to think of the best polyglots out there, people that speak thirty or more languages and even use them daily at work. Visualize them having the same problems you're having right now. Project your struggles upon them. Know that they had all these exact problems at some point.

All these experts, all these… superhumans, were once beginners like you and me. They knew just as many things as you and I do about a new language. They even felt the same way as you do now, yet they kept learning.

That's exactly what I did too, and that's how I learned several languages.

We're all in this together. The difference is that some quit, and others keep going. It's easy to figure out which group becomes fluent and which doesn't.

So if there's anything you should keep from this book, it's what I call the Key Phrases of Language Learning:

- Be patient.
- You'll get used to it.
- Keep trying and failing until someday you no longer fail.

Even if you forget the same word for the tenth time, even if you can't string a sentence in the language together, even if somebody told you you'll never learn any language, even if you made an embarrassing mistake that cost you a lot …

Keep learning.

You'll become fluent. You'll prove the naysayers wrong, even yourself. You'll reach milestones you never thought were possible for you to reach—as long as you don't quit when others do.

I can't tell you how many times I've said, "I'll never learn that language." Yet I know it's just me whining, so I keep learning until one day, I realize I'm way better than I was before.

Life has been very kind to me every time I kept going, no matter what. In contrast, life wasn't so kind every time I quit. I know which one I prefer. Do you?

If something about a language seems too hard for you to learn or understand, choose to learn other aspects in the language and get back to it later. I promise you everything will eventually fall into place. When you're least expecting it, you'll understand what's happening.

Language learning is a choice. Make that choice every day, and you'll see results—maybe not as fast as you want, but trust me ... they'll come.

It's all about the daily choices you make. So choose to learn something today!

Happy language learning,
Maria

CAN YOU HELP?

Thank You For Reading My Book!

I really appreciate all of your feedback, and I love hearing what you have to say.

I need your input to make the next version of this book and my future books better.

Please leave me an honest review on Amazon letting me know what you thought of the book.

Thanks so much!

Maria Spantidi